DK EYEWITNESS TRAVEL

15-MINUTE
FRENCH

LEARN FRENCH
IN JUST 15
MINUTES A DAY

CAROLINE LEMOINE

D0001090

DK

London, New York, Munich, Melbourne, and Delhi

Dorling Kindersley Limited
Senior Editor Angeles Gavira
Project Art Editor Vanessa Marr
DTP Designer John Goldsmid
Production Controller Luca Frassinetti
Publishing Manager Liz Wheeler
Managing Art Editor Philip Ormerod
Publishing Director Jonathan Metcalf
Art Director Bryn Walls

Language content for Dorling Kindersley by
g-and-w publishing

Produced for Dorling Kindersley by
Schermuly Design Co.
Art Editor Hugh Schermuly
Project Editor Cathy Meeus
Special photography Mike Good

First American Edition, 2005
Published in the United States by
DK Publishing, Inc., 375 Hudson Street,
New York, New York 10014

05 06 07 08 09   10 9 8 7 6 5 4 3 2

A Cataloging-in-Publication record for this book
is available from the Library of Congress.

ISBN 0-7566-0922-4

15-Minute French is also available in a pack
with two CDs (ISBN 0-7566-0931-3)

Color reproduction by Colourscan, Singapore
Printed and bound in China by Leo Paper
Products Limited

Discover more at
www.dk.com

Contents

How to use this book

This main part of the book is devoted to 12 themed chapters, broken down into five 15-minute daily lessons, the last of which is a revision lesson. So, in just 12 weeks you will have completed the course. A concluding reference section contains a menu guide and English-to-French and French-to-English dictionaries.

Warm up and clock
Each day starts with a one-minute warm-up that encourages you to recall vocabulary or phrases you have learned previously. A clock to the right of the heading bar indicates the amount of time you are expected to spend on each exercise.

Instructions
Each exercise is numbered and introduced by instructions that explain what to do. In some cases additional information is given about the language point being covered.

Cultural/Conversational tip
These panels provide additional insights into life in France and language usage.

Text styles
Distinctive text styles differentiate French and English, and the pronunciation guide (see right).

In conversation
Illustrated dialogues reflecting how vocabulary and phrases are used in everyday situations appear throughout the book.

How to use the flap
The book's cover flaps allow you to conceal the French so that you can test whether you have remembered correctly.

Review and repeat
A recap of selected elements of previous lessons helps to reinforce your knowledge.

Useful phrases
Selected phrases relevant to the topic help you speak and understand.

EATING AND DRINKING 19

Useful phrases

Learn these phrases. Read the English under the pictures and say the phrase in French as shown on the right. Then conceal the French with the cover flap and test yourself.

le pain
luh pañ
bread

Je voudrais un grand café, s'il vous plaît.
juh voodray uñ grañ kafay, seel voo play

I'd like a large black coffee, please.

C'est tout?
say too

Is that all?

Je prends un croissant.
juh prañ uñ krwasoñ

I'll have a croissant.

le café au lait
luh kafay oh lay
large coffee with milk

C'est combien?
say kõbyañ

How much is that?

Oui, bien sûr.
wee, byañ sur
Yes, certainly.

Alors deux croissants. C'est combien?
alor duh krwasoñ. say kõbyañ

Two croissants, then. How much is that?

Quatre euros, s'il vous plaît.
katruh uroh, seel voo play

Four euros, please.

Pronunciation guide

Many French sounds will already be familiar to you, but a few require special attention. Take note of how these letters are pronounced:

r a French **r** is pronounced in the back of the throat, producing a sound a little like gargling

j a French **j** is soft like the sound in the middle of *pleasure* (as opposed to the hard English *j* as in *major*)

n **n** is pronounced nasally when in the combination **on**, **an** or **in**. Imagine saying *huh* through your nose. The nasal **n** is shown in the pronunciation with this symbol: ñ

ch ch in French is equivalent to *sh* in English, as in *ship*

er/ez these endings are pronounced ay as in *play*

Pay attention also to these vowel sounds as they may vary from English:

i as the English *keep*
au as the English *over*
eu as the English *fur*
oi as the English *wag*

Below each French word or phrase you will find a pronunciation transcription. Read this, bearing in mind the tips above, and you will achieve a comprehensible result. But remember that the transcription can only ever be an approximation and that there is no real substitute for listening to and mimicking native speakers.

Say it
In these exercises you are asked to apply what you have learned using different vocabulary.

5 Say it

Do you have a single room?

For six nights.

Does it have a balcony?

Dictionary
A mini-dictionary provides ready reference from English to French and French to English for 2,500 words.

128 DICTIONARY

Dictionary
English to French

The gender of a French noun (singular) is indicated by the words for *the*: **le** and **la** (masculine and feminine). If these are abbreviated to *l'* in front of a vowel or the letter "h" or if the noun is plural, indicated by **les**, then the gender is indicated by the abbreviations "(m)" or "(f)." French adjectives (adj) vary according to the gender and number of the word they describe; the masculine form is shown here. In most cases, you add **-e** to the masculine form to make it feminine. Certain endings use a different rule: masculine adjectives that end in **-x** adopt an **-se** ending in the feminine form, while those that end in **-eu** change to **-euse**. Some feminine adjectives that do not follow these rules are shown here and follow the abbreviation "(fem)." For the plural form, **-s** is usually added.

Menu guide
Use this guide as a reference for food terminology and popular French dishes.

128 MENU GUIDE

Menu guide

This guide lists the most common terms you may encounter on French menus or when shopping for food. If you can't find an exact phrase, try looking up its component parts.

Bonjour
Hello

In France it is part of the culture to greet family and friends with kisses on the cheek. The number of kisses varies from two to four. For example, it is usually three kisses in the south but two in Brittany. In more formal situations, a handshake is part of the normal greeting.

2 Words to remember

Look at these polite expressions and say them aloud. Cover the text on the left with the cover flap and try to remember the French for each item. Check your answers.

Salut!
saloo
Hi!

Bonjour. boñjoor	*Hello.*
Bonsoir/bonne nuit. boñswar/bon nwee	*Good evening/good night.*
Je m'appelle Jean. juh mapell joñ	*My name is Jean.*
Enchanté *(men)/* **Enchantée** *(women).* oñshontay	*Pleased to meet you.*

🇫🇷 **Cultural tip** The French tend to greet people with "monsieur" (sir), "madame" (madam, for older women), or "mademoiselle" (miss, for younger women) much more than most English-speakers would.

3 In conversation: formal

Bonjour. Je m'appelle Céline Legrand.
boñjoor. juh mapell seleen luhgroñ

Hello. My name is Céline Legrand.

Bonjour madame. Monsieur Rossi, enchanté.
boñjoor ma-dam. musyuh rossee, oñshontay

Hello (madam). Mr. Rossi, pleased to meet you.

Enchantée.
oñshontay

Pleased to meet you.

4 Put into practice

Join in this conversation. Read the French beside the pictures on the left and then follow the instructions to make your reply. Then test yourself by concealing the answers on the right with the cover flap.

Bonjour monsieur.
boñjoor musyuh.
Hello, sir.

Say: Hello,
mademoiselle.

**Bonjour
mademoiselle.**
boñjoor mad-mwazel

Je m'appelle Martine.
juh mapell marteen.
My name is Martine.

Say: Pleased to meet
you.

Enchanté.
oñshontay

5 Useful phrases

Familiarize yourself with these phrases. Read them aloud several times and try to memorize them. Conceal the French with the cover flap and test yourself.

Goodbye.	**Au revoir.** ovwar
See you soon.	**A bientôt.** ah byañtoe
See you tomorrow.	**A demain.** ah dumañ
Thank you (very much).	**Merci (beaucoup).** mairsee (bohkoo)

6 In conversation: informal

Alors, à demain?
alor, ah dumañ

So, see you tomorrow?

Oui, au revoir.
wee, ovwar

Yes, goodbye.

Au revoir. A bientôt.
ovwar. ah byañtoe

Goodbye. See you soon.

Les relations
Relatives

1 Warm up

Say "hello" and "goodbye" in French. (pp.8–9)

Now say "My name is…" (pp.8–9)

Say "sir" and "madam." (pp.8–9)

In French, the same word is used for relationships by marriage: **beau-père** means both father-in-law and step-father, and **belle-fille** means daughter-in-law and stepdaughter. The French for *the* is **le** or **la**, and *a* is **un** or **une**, depending on whether the word is masculine or feminine (see below).

2 Match and repeat

Look at the people in this scene and match their numbers with the vocabulary list at the side. Read the French words aloud. Then cover the list with the flap and test yourself.

1 **le grand-père**
  luh groñpair

2 **le frère**
  luh frair

3 **la sœur**
  lah sur

4 **le père**
  luh pair

5 **la mère**
  lah mair

6 **la grand-mère**
  lah groñmair

7 **le fils**
  luh fees

8 **la fille**
  lah feeyuh

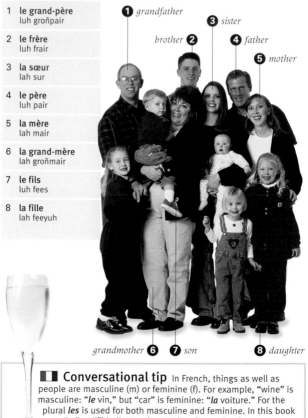

❶ grandfather
❷ brother
❸ sister
❹ father
❺ mother
grandmother ❻ ❼ son ❽ daughter

🏳 **Conversational tip** In French, things as well as people are masculine (m) or feminine (f). For example, "wine" is masculine: "*le* vin," but "car" is feminine: "*la* voiture." For the plural *les* is used for both masculine and feminine. In this book "m" or "f" indicates the gender after a plural.

3 Words to remember: relatives

Look at these words and say them aloud. Conceal the text on the right with the cover flap and try to remember the French. Check your answers. Then practice the phrases below.

le mari   **la femme**
luh maree   lah fam
husband   *wife*

Nous sommes mariés.
Noo som mareeay
We are married.

sister-in-law/ stepsister	**la belle-sœur** lah bell sur
brother-in-law/ stepbrother	**le beau-frère** luh boe frair
half-sister	**la demi-sœur** lah dumee sur
half-brother	**le demi-frère** luh dumee frair
children	**les enfants (m)** lay zoñfoñ
I have four children.	**J'ai quatre enfants.** jay katruh oñfoñ
I have two stepdaughters.	**J'ai deux belles-filles.** jay duh bell feeyuh

4 Words to remember: numbers

Memorize these words. Now cover the French and test yourself.

Be careful with the pronunciation of **deux** and **trois**. When you say them in front of a word that starts with a vowel, you need to say an extra "z" sound—for example, **deux enfants** (*two children*) is pronounced duh zoñfoñ, and **trois éclairs** (*three eclairs*), trwah zayclair. This is also true of other words.

one	**un/une** uñ *(m)*/oon *(f)*
two	**deux** duh
three	**trois** trwah
four	**quatre** katruh
five	**cinq** sank
six	**six** sees
seven	**sept** set
eight	**huit** weet
nine	**neuf** nurf
ten	**dix** dees

5 Say it

I have five sons.

I have three sisters and a brother.

I have two stepsons.

1 Warm up

Say the French for as many members of the family as you can. (pp.10–11)

Say "I have two sons." (pp.10–11)

Ma famille
My family

The French have two ways of saying "you": **vous** for people you meet or don't know very well and **tu** for family and friends. Similarly, there are different words for "your." The words for "my" and "your" also change depending on whether they relate to masculine, feminine, or plural nouns.

2 Words to remember

Say these words out loud a few times. Cover the French with the flap and try to remember the French word for each item.

mon moñ	*my (with masculine)*
ma mah	*my (with feminine)*
mes may	*my (with plural)*
ton toñ	*your (informal, with masculine)*
ta tah	*your (informal, with feminine)*
tes tay	*your (informal, with plural)*
votre votruh	*your (formal, with masculine or feminine)*
vos voe	*your (formal, with plural)*

Voici mes parents.
vwasee may paroñ
These are my parents.

3 In conversation

Vous avez des enfants?
voo zavay day zoñfoñ

Do you have any children?

Oui, j'ai deux filles.
wee, jay duh feeyuh

Yes, I have two daughters.

Voici mes filles. Et vous?
vwasee may feeyuh.
ay voo

These are my daughters. And you?

Conversational tip The French usually ask a question by simply raising the pitch of the voice at the end of a statement—for example, "Vous voulez un café?" ("Do you want coffee?"). You could also ask the same question by inverting the verb and subject: "Voulez-vous un café?". Or you can put "Est-ce que" in front of the sentence: "Est-ce que vous voulez un café?"

4 Useful phrases

Read these phrases aloud several times and try to memorize them. Conceal the French with the cover flap and test yourself.

	Do you have any brothers? (formal)	**Vous avez des frères?** voo zavay day frair
	Do you have any brothers? (informal)	**Tu as des frères?** tew ah day frair
	This is my husband.	**Voici mon mari.** vwasee moñ maree
	That's my wife.	**C'est ma femme.** say mah fam
	Is that your sister? (formal)	**C'est votre sœur?** say votruh sur
	Is that your sister? (informal)	**C'est ta sœur?** say tah sur

J'ai un beau-fils.
jay uñ boe fees

I have a stepson.

5 Say it

Do you have any brothers and sisters? (formal)

Do you have any children? (informal)

I have two sisters.

This is my wife.

1 Warm up

Say "See you soon."
(pp.8–9)

Say "I am married"
(pp.10–11) and
"I have a daughter."
(pp.12–13)

Etre et avoir
To be and to have

There are some essential verbs for you to learn in this course. You can use these to construct a large variety of useful phrases. The first two are **être** (*to be*) and **avoir** (*to have*). Learn them carefully, since French verbs change more than English ones according to the pronoun (I, you, etc.) used.

2 Etre: to be

Familiarize yourself with the different forms of **être** (*to be*). Use the cover flaps to test yourself and, when you are confident, practice the sample sentences below.

je suis juh swee	*I am*
tu es tew ay	*you are (informal singular)*
il/elle est eel/el ay	*he/she is*
nous sommes noo som	*we are*
vous êtes voo zet	*you are (formal singular or plural)*
ils/elles sont eel/el soñ	*they are*

Je suis anglaise.
juh swee zonglayz
I'm English.

Je suis fatigué(e). juh swee fatigay	*I'm tired.*
Vous êtes à l'heure. voo zet ah lur	*You're on time.*
Elle est heureuse? el ay tururz	*Is she happy?*
Nous sommes français. noo som froñsay	*We're French.*

3 Avoir: to have

Practice **avoir** (*to have*) and the sample sentences, then test yourself.

I have	**j'ai** jay
you have (informal singular)	**tu as** tew ah
he/she has	**il/elle a** eel/el ah
we have	**nous avons** noo zavoñ
you have (formal singular or plural)	**vous avez** voo zavay
they have	**ils/elles ont** eel/el zoñ

Il a deux baguettes.
eel ah duh baget
He has two baguettes.

He has a meeting.	**Il a un rendez-vous.** eel ah uñ roñday-voo
Do you have a cell phone?	**Vous avez un portable?** voo zavay uñ portabluh
How many brothers and sisters do you have?	**Vous avez combien de frères et sœurs?** voo zavay koñbyañ duh frair ay sur

4 Negatives

To make a sentence negative in French, put **ne** in front of the verb and **pas** just after: **nous ne sommes pas anglais** (*we are not English*). If **ne** is followed by a vowel, it becomes **n'**: **je n'ai pas d'enfants** (*I don't have any children*). But many French people drop the **ne** when they're talking, so you'll just hear **nous sommes pas** (*we aren't*), **j'ai pas** (*I haven't*), and so on. Read these sentences aloud, then cover the French with the flap and test yourself.

le vélo
luh vayloe
bicycle

He's not married.	**Il n'est pas marié.** eel nay pah mariyay
I am not sure.	**Je ne suis pas sûr(e).** juh nuh swee pah syur
We don't have any children.	**Nous n'avons pas d'enfants.** noo navoñ pah doñfoñ

Je n'ai pas de voiture.
juh nay pas duh vwatyur
I don't have a car.

Réponses
Answers
Cover with flap

Révisez et répétez
Review and repeat

1 How many?

1 **trois**
trwah

2 **neuf**
nurf

3 **quatre**
katruh

4 **deux**
duh

5 **huit**
weet

6 **dix**
dees

7 **cinq**
sank

8 **sept**
set

9 **six**
sees

1 How many?

Cover the answers with the flap. Then say these French numbers out loud. Check that you have remembered the French correctly.

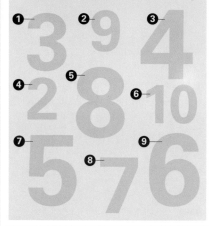

2 Hello

1 **Bonjour. Je m'appelle... [your name].**
boñjoor. juh mapell...

2 **Enchanté(e).**
oñshontay

3 **Oui, et j'ai deux fils. Et vous?**
wee, ay jay duh fees. ay voo

4 **Au revoir. A demain.**
ovwar. ah dumañ

2 Hello

You meet someone in a formal situation. Join in the conversation, replying in French according to the English prompts.

Bonjour. Je m'appelle Nicole.
1 *Answer the greeting and give your name.*

Voici mon mari, Henri.
2 *Say "Pleased to meet you."*

Vous êtes marié(e)?
3 *Say "Yes, and I have two sons. And you?"*

Nous avons trois filles.
4 *Say "Goodbye. See you tomorrow."*

3 To have or be

Fill in the blanks with the correct form of
avoir (*to have*) or **être** (*to be*). Check that you
have remembered the French correctly.

1 Je _____ anglaise.

2 Nous _____ quatre enfants.

3 Elle _____ une belle-fille.

4 Vous _____ rendez-vous?

5 Il n' _____ pas fatigué.

6 Je n' _____ pas de
portable.

7 Tu n' _____ pas
sûr?

8 Nous _____
français.

3 To have or be

1 **suis**
swee

2 **avons**
avoñ

3 **a**
ah

4 **avez**
avay

5 **est**
ay

6 **ai**
ay

7 **es**
ay

8 **sommes**
som

4 Family

Say the French for each of the numbered
family members. Check that you have
remembered the French correctly.

grandfather **1**
brother **2**
3 sister
4 father
5 mother
grandmother **6** **7** son
8 daughter

4 Family

1 **le grand-père**
luh groñpair

2 **le frère**
luh frair

3 **la soeur**
lah sur

4 **le père**
luh pair

5 **la mère**
lah mair

6 **la grand-mère**
lah groñmair

7 **le fils**
luh fees

8 **la fille**
lah feeyuh

1 Warm up

Count to ten
(pp.10–11).

Remind yourself how
to say "hello" and
"goodbye." (pp.8–9)

Ask "Do you have a
baguette?" (pp.14–15)

Au café
In the café

In a typical French café you can either
sit at the counter, which is cheaper,
or have waiter service at a table.
Tipping is the norm if you're happy
with the service, but a few coins will
be enough. Food is not usually served,
although you can often get bread and
croissants in the mornings.

2 Words to remember

Look at the words below and say them out
loud a few times. Cover the French with the
flap and try to remember the French for each
item. Practice the words on the picture also.

le café crème luh kafay krem	*coffee with frothy milk*
le grand café luh groñ kafay	*large black coffee*
le thé luh tay	*black tea*
le thé au lait luh tay oh lay	*tea with milk*

la confiture
lah coñfeetyur
jam

le café
luh cafeh
small black coffee

le sucre
luh sookruh
sugar

■ Cultural tip A standard coffee is small and black.
You'll need to ask if you want it any other way. If you like
milk in your tea, you'll need to specify cold milk ("lait froid"/
lay frwah), otherwise you are likely to get a jug of hot milk.

3 In conversation

**Bonjour. Je voudrais
un café au lait, s'il
vous plaît.**
bonjoor. juh voodray uñ
kafay oh lay, seel voo
play

*Hello. I would like
coffee with milk, please.*

C'est tout madame?
say too ma-dam

Is that all, madam?

**Vous avez des
croissants?**
voo zavay day krossoñ

*Do you have any
croissants?*

le pain
luh pañ
bread

le café au lait
luh kafay oh lay
large coffee with milk

4 Useful phrases

Learn these phrases. Read the English under the pictures and say the phrase in French as shown on the right. Then conceal the French with the cover flap and test yourself.

I'd like a large black coffee, please.

Je voudrais un grand café, s'il vous plaît.
juh voodray uñ groñ kafay, seel voo play

Is that all?

C'est tout?
say too

I'll have a croissant.

Je prends un croissant.
juh pron uñ krossoñ

How much is that?

C'est combien?
say koñbyañ

Oui, bien sûr.
wee, byañ syur

Yes, certainly.

Alors deux croissants.
C'est combien?
alor duh krossoñ. say koñbyañ

Two croissants, then.
How much is that?

Quatre euros, s'il vous plaît.
katruh uroh, seel voo play

Four euros, please.

Say "I'd like..."
(pp.18–19)

Say "I don't have a
brother." (pp.14–15)

Ask "Do you have any
croissants?"
(pp.18–19)

Au restaurant
In the restaurant

There is a variety of different types of
eating places in France. In a **café** you
can find a few snacks. A **brasserie** is
a traditional restaurant; the service is
fast and there's usually no need to
make reservations. In the more formal
gastronomic restaurants, it is
necessary to book and to dress up.

2 Words to remember

Memorize these words. Conceal the French
with the cover flap and test yourself.

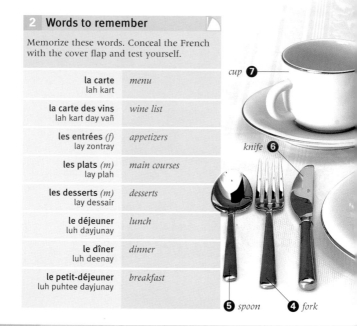

la carte lah kart	*menu*
la carte des vins lah kart day vañ	*wine list*
les entrées *(f)* lay zontray	*appetizers*
les plats *(m)* lay plah	*main courses*
les desserts *(m)* lay dessair	*desserts*
le déjeuner luh dayjunay	*lunch*
le dîner luh deenay	*dinner*
le petit-déjeuner luh puhtee dayjunay	*breakfast*

cup **7**

knife **6**

5 *spoon*   **4** *fork*

3 In conversation

**Bonjour. Je voudrais
une table pour quatre.**
boñjoor. juh voodray
oon tabluh poor katruh

*Hello. I would like a
table for four.*

**Vous avez une
réservation?**
voo zavay oon
raysairvasyoñ

*Do you have a
reservation?*

Oui, au nom de Smith.
wee, oh noñ duh Smith

*Yes, in the name
of Smith.*

4 Match and repeat

Look at the numbered items in this table setting and match them with the French words on the right. Read the French words aloud. Now, conceal the French with the cover flap and test yourself.

glass **1**

8 *saucer*

1 **le verre**
luh vair

2 **la serviette**
lah sairvyet

3 **l'assiette** *(f)*
lasyet

4 **la fourchette**
lah forshet

5 **la cuillère**
lah kweeyair

6 **le couteau**
luh kootoe

7 **la tasse**
lah tass

8 **la soucoupe**
lah sookoop

napkin **2**

plate **3**

5 Useful phrases

Learn these phrases and then test yourself using the cover flap to conceal the French.

What do you have for dessert?	**Qu'est ce que vous avez comme dessert?** keskuh voo zavay kom dessair
The check, please.	**L'addition, s'il vous plaît.** ladeesyoñ, seel voo play

D'accord. Quelle table vous préférez?
dakor. kel tabluh voo prayfayray

Fine. Which table would you like?

Près de la fenêtre, s'il vous plaît.
pray duh lah fenetruh, seel voo play

Near the window, please.

Mais bien sûr. Suivez-moi.
may byañ syur. sweevay mwah

Of course. Follow me.

Vouloir
To want

In this section, you will learn the present tense of a verb that is essential to everyday conversation—**vouloir** (*to want*)—as well as a useful polite form, **je voudrais** (*I would like*). Remember to use this form when requesting something because **je veux** (*I want*) may sound too strong.

2 Vouloir: to want

Say the different forms of **vouloir** (*to want*) aloud. Use the cover flaps to test yourself and, when you are confident, practice the sample sentences below.

je veux juh vuh	*I want*
tu veux tew vuh	*you want (informal)*
il/elle veut eel/el vuh	*he/she wants*
nous voulons noo vooloñ	*we want*
vous voulez voo voolay	*you want (formal/plural)*
ils/elles veulent eel/el verl	*they want*
Tu veux du vin? tew vuh dew vañ	*Do you want some wine?*
Elle veut une nouvelle voiture. el vuh oon noovel vwatyur	*She wants a new car.*
Nous voulons aller en vacances. noo vooloñ zallay oñ vakons	*We want to go on vacation.*

Je veux des bonbons.
juh vuh day boñ-boñ
I want some candy.

Conversational tip To say "some," "de" ("of") combines with "le," "la," or "les" to produce "du" for the masculine, "de la" for feminine, or "des" for the plural, as in "du café," "de la confiture," and "des citrons" (lemons). If the sentence is negative, use only "de," as in "Il n'y a pas de café." In the same way, à ("to") combines with "le," "la," or "les" to produce "au" for the masculine, "à la" for the feminine, and "aux" for the plural.

3 Polite requests

There is a form of **je veux** (*I want*) used for polite requests: **je voudrais**. Practice the sentences below and then test yourself.

I'd like a beer, please.

Je voudrais une bière, s'il vous plaît.
juh voodray oon biyair, seel voo play

I'd like a table for tonight.

Je voudrais une table pour ce soir.
juh voodray oon tabluh poor suh swar

I'd like the menu.

Je voudrais la carte.
juh voodray lah kart

4 Put into practice

Join in this conversation. Read the French beside the pictures on the left and then follow the English prompts to make your reply in French. Test yourself by concealing the answers with the cover flap.

Bonsoir, madame. Vous avez une réservation?
boñswar, ma-dam. Voo zavay oon raysairvasyoñ
Good evening, madam. Do you have a reservation?

Say: No, but I would like a table for three, please.

Non, mais je voudrais une table pour trois, s'il vous plaît.
noñ, may juh voodray oon tabluh poor trwah, seel voo play

Fumeur ou non-fumeur?
foomur oo noñ-foomur
Smoking or nonsmoking?

Say: I'd like nonsmoking, please.

Je voudrais non-fumeur, s'il vous plaît.
juh voodray noñ-foomur, seel voo play

Les plats
Dishes

France is famous for its cuisine and the quality of its best restaurants. It also offers a wide variety of regional dishes. Plenty of garlic and butter are a feature of many typical dishes. Although traditionally French cuisine is meat-based, many restaurants now offer a vegetarian menu.

1 Warm up

Say "I'm tired" and "I'm not sure." (pp.14–15)

Ask "Do you have croissants?" (pp.18–19)

Say "I'd like a white coffee." (pp.18–19)

🇫🇷 **Cultural tip** You will usually have the choice of eating a set "menu" or ordering "à la carte." With a set menu, salad is often a starter and you usually have to choose between dessert or cheese.

2 Match and repeat

Look at the numbered items and match them to the French words in the panel on the left. Test yourself using the cover flap.

1 **les légumes** *(m)*
lay laygoom

2 **le fruit**
luh froo-wee

3 **le fromage**
luh fromarj

4 **les noix** *(f)*
lay nwah

5 **la soupe**
lah soop

6 **la volaille**
lah vol-eye

7 **le poisson**
luh pwassoñ

8 **les pâtes** *(f)*
lay pat

9 **les fruits de mer** *(m)*
lay froo-wee
duh mair

10 **la viande**
lah vee-ond

❶ *vegetables*

❷ *fruit*

cheese ❸

❺ *soup*   *poultry* ❻

❽ *pasta*   ❾ *seafood*

3 Words to remember: cooking methods

Familiarize yourself with these words and then test yourself.

**Je voudrais mon steak
bien cuit.**
juh voodray moñ stayk
byañ kwee
*I'd like my steak
well done.*

fried	**frit(e)**	free(t)
grilled	**grillé(e)**	greeyay
roasted	**rôti(e)**	rotee
boiled	**bouilli(e)**	booyee
steamed	**à la vapeur**	ah lah vapur
rare	**saignant(e)**	say-nyoñ(t)

6 Say it

What is "cassoulet"?

I'm allergic to
seafood.

I'd like a beer.

4 *nuts*

4 Words to remember: drinks

Familiarize yourself with these words.

water	**l'eau** *(f)*	loe
fizzy water	**l'eau gazeuse** *(f)*	loe gazuz
still water	**l'eau plate** *(f)*	loe plat
wine	**le vin**	luh vañ
beer	**la bière**	lah biyair
fruit juice	**le jus de fruits**	luh joo duh froo-wee

7 *fish*

5 Useful phrases

Learn these phrases and then test yourself.

I'm a vegetarian.	**Je suis végétarien.** juh swee vejitah-ryañ
I'm allergic to nuts.	**Je suis allergique aux noix.** juh swee zalurzheek oh nwah
What are "escargots"?	**Qu'est que c'est les "escargots"?** keskuh say lay zeskargoh

10 *meat*

Révisez et répétez
Review and repeat

Réponses
Answers
Cover with flap

1 At the table

1 **les noix**
lay nwah

2 **les fruits de mer**
lay froo-wee
duh mair

3 **la viande**
lah vee-ond

4 **le sucre**
luh sookruh

5 **le verre**
luh vair

1 At the table

Name the numbered items.

1 nuts
2 seafood
3 meat
4 sugar
5 glass

2 This is my...

1 **C'est mon mari.**
say moñ maree

2 **Voici ma fille.**
vwasee mah feeyuh

3 **Ma table est
non-fumeur.**
mah tabluh ay noñ-
foomur

4 **Mes enfants
sont fatigués.**
may zoñfoñ soñ
fatigay

2 This is my...

Say these phrases in French.
Use **mon**, **ma**, or **mes**.

1 *This is my husband.*

2 *Here is my daughter.*

3 *My table is nonsmoking.*

4 *My children are tired.*

3 I'd like...

1 **Je voudrais un
café.**
juh voodray uñ
kafay

2 **Je voudrais de la
confiture.**
juh voodray duh
lah coñfeetyur

3 **Je voudrais du
pain.**
juh voodray doo
pañ

4 **Je voudrais un
café au lait.**
juh voodray uñ
kafay oh lay

3 I'd like...

Say you'd like the following:

1 black coffee
2 jam
3 bread
4 large coffee
with milk

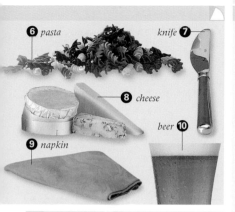

6 *pasta*

knife 7

8 *cheese*

beer 10

9 *napkin*

1 At the table

6 **les pâtes**
lay pat

7 **le couteau**
luh kootoe

8 **le fromage**
luh fromarj

9 **la serviette**
lah sairvyet

10 **la bière**
lah biyair

4 Restaurant

You arrive at a restaurant. Join in the conversation, replying in French according to the English prompts.

Bonjour madame, monsieur.
1 *Ask for a table for six.*

Fumeur ou non-fumeur?
2 *Say: nonsmoking.*

Suivez-moi, s'il vous plaît.
3 *Ask for the menu.*

Et vous voulez la carte des vins?
4 *Say: No. Sparkling water, please.*

Voilà.
5 *Say: I don't have a glass.*

4 Restaurant

1 **Bonjour. Je voudrais une table pour six.**
boñjoor. juh voodray oon tabluh por sees

2 **Non-fumeur.**
noñ-foomur

3 **La carte, s'il vous plaît.**
lah kart, seel voo play

4 **Non. De l'eau gazeuse, s'il vous plaît,**
noñ. duh loe gazuz, seel voo play

5 **Je n'ai pas de verre.**
juh nay pah duh vair

1 Warm up

Say "he is" and "they are." (pp.14–15)

Say "he is not" and "they are not." (pp.14–15)

What is French for "the children"? (pp.10–11)

Les jours et les mois
Days and months

In French, the days of the week (**les jours de semaine**) and months (**les mois**) are not capitalized. The months have names similar to the English ones. You use **en** with months: **en avril** (*in April*), but not with days.

2 Words to remember: days

Familiarize yourself with these words and test yourself using the flap.

lundi luñdee	*Monday*	
mardi mardee	*Tuesday*	
mercredi mairkrudee	*Wednesday*	
jeudi jurdee	*Thursday*	
vendredi voñdrudee	*Friday*	
samedi samdee	*Saturday*	
dimanche deemonsh	*Sunday*	
aujourd'hui oh-joordwee	*today*	
demain dumañ	*tomorrow*	
hier eeyair	*yesterday*	

Demain, c'est lundi.
dumañ, say luñdee
Tomorrow is Monday.

3 Useful phrases: days

Learn these phrases and then test yourself using the cover flap.

La réunion n'est pas mardi. lah rayoonyoñ nay pah mardee	*The meeting isn't on Tuesday.*	
Je travaille le dimanche. juh trav-eye luh deemonsh	*I work on Sundays.*	

4 Words to remember: months

Familiarize yourself with these words and test yourself using the flap.

Notre anniversaire de mariage est en juillet.
notruh aneevairsair duh
mareeaj ay toñ jweeyay
*Our wedding
anniversary is in July.*

January	**janvier**	joñvyay
February	**février**	fevreeyay
March	**mars**	mars
April	**avril**	avreel
May	**mai**	may
June	**juin**	jwañ
July	**juillet**	jweeyay
August	**août**	oot
September	**septembre**	septombruh
October	**octobre**	oktobruh
November	**novembre**	novombruh
December	**décembre**	daysombruh
month	**le mois**	luh mwah
year	**l'an** *(m)*	loñ

Noël est en dècembre.
nowel ay toñ daysombruh
*Christmas is in
December.*

5 Useful phrases: months

Learn these phrases and then test yourself using the cover flap.

*My children are on
vacation in August.*
**Mes enfants sont en
vacances en août.**
may zoñfoñ soñ toñ
vakons oñ oot

*My birthday is
in June.*
**Mon anniversaire est
en juin.**
moñ naneevairsair ay
toñ jwañ

1 Warm up

Count in French from
1 to 10. (pp.10–11)

Say "I have a
reservation."
(pp.20–1)

Say "The meeting is
on Wednesday."
(pp.28–9)

L'heure et les nombres
Time and numbers

The 12-hour clock is used in everyday
speech, while the 24-hour clock is
employed in bus stations, airports, etc.
Where the minutes are first in English
(*ten to five*), in French the hour is first:
dix heures moins cinq (*ten minus five*).

2 Words to remember: time

Memorize how to tell the time in French.

une heure oon ur	*one o'clock*
une heure cinq oon ur sank	*five after one*
une heure et quart oon ur ay kar	*quarter after one*
une heure vingt oon ur vañ	*one-twenty*
une heure et demie oon ur ay dumee	*one-thirty*
deux heures moins le quart duh zur mwañ luh kar	*quarter to two*
deux heures moins dix duh zur mwañ dees	*ten to two*

3 Useful phrases

Learn these phrases and then test yourself using the cover flap.

Quelle heure est-il? kel ur ay teel	*What time is it?*
A quelle heure voulez-vous le petit déjeuner? ah kel ur voolay voo luh puhtee dayjunay	*What time do you want breakfast?*
J'ai une réservation pour douze heures. jay oon raysairvasyoñ poor dooz ur	*I have a reservation for twelve o'clock.*

4 Words to remember: higher numbers

In French when you say 21, 31, etc. you say: **vingt-et-un**, **trente-et-un**, and so on. After that, just put the numbers together without "et": **vingt-deux** (22), **quarante-cinq** (45).

Seventy is **soixante-dix** (*sixty-ten*), 75 is **soixante-quinze** (*sixty-fifteen*), and so on. **Quatre-vingt** (80) means *four-twenties*, and 90 is **quatre-vingt-dix** (*four-twenties-ten*). So 82 is **quatre-vingt-deux** and 97 is **quatre-vingt-dix-sept**.

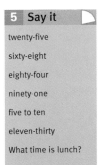

Ça fait quatre-vingt-cinq euros.
sah fay katruh-vañ-sank uroh
That's eighty-five euros.

eleven	**onze**	onz
twelve	**douze**	dooz
thirteen	**treize**	trez
fourteen	**quatorze**	katorz
fifteen	**quinze**	kanz
sixteen	**seize**	sez
seventeen	**dix-sept**	deeset
eighteen	**dix-huit**	deezweet
nineteen	**dix-neuf**	deeznurf
twenty	**vingt**	vañ
thirty	**trente**	tront
forty	**quarante**	karont
fifty	**cinquante**	sankont
sixty	**soixante**	swasont
seventy	**soixante-dix**	swasont-dees
eighty	**quatre-vingt**	katruh-vañ
ninety	**quatre-vingt-dix**	katruh-vañ-dees
one hundred	**cent**	soñ
three hundred	**trois cents**	trwah soñ
one thousand	**mille**	meel
ten thousand	**dix mille**	dee meel
two hundred thousand	**deux cent mille**	duh soñ meel
one million	**un million**	oon meel-yoñ

5 Say it

twenty-five

sixty-eight

eighty-four

ninety-one

five to ten

eleven-thirty

What time is lunch?

1 Warm up

Say the days of the week. (pp.28–9)

Say "It's three o'clock." (pp.30–1)

What's the French for "today," "tomorrow," and "yesterday"? (pp.28–9)

Les rendez-vous
Appointments

Business in France is generally conducted more formally than in the United States; always address your business contacts as **vous**. The French tend to leave the office for the lunch hour, often having a sit-down meal in a restaurant or, less commonly, at home.

2 Useful phrases

Learn these phrases and then test yourself.

Prenons rendez-vous pour demain. prunoñ ronday-voo poor dumañ	*Let's meet tomorrow.*
Avec qui? avek kee	*With whom?*
Quand êtes-vous libre? koñ et-voo leebruh	*When are you free?*
Je suis désolé(e), je suis occupé(e). juh swee dayzolay, juh swee zokupay	*I'm sorry, I'm busy.*
Pourquoi pas jeudi? poorkwah pah jurdee	*How about Thursday?*
C'est bon pour moi. say boh poor mwah	*That's good for me.*

la poignée de main
lah pwanyay duh mañ
handshake

Bienvenue.
byañvenoo
Welcome.

3 In conversation

Bonjour. J'ai rendez-vous.
boñjoor. jay ronday-voo

Hello. I have an appointment.

Avec qui?
avek kee

With whom?

Avec Monsieur Le Blanc.
avek musyuh luh bloñ

With Mr. Le Blanc.

4 Put into practice

Join in this conversation. Read the French beside the pictures on the left and then follow the instructions to make your reply. Then test yourself by concealing the answers on the right with the cover flap.

Prenons rendez-vous pour jeudi.
prunoñ ronday-voo poor jurdee
Let's meet on Thursday.

Say: Sorry, I'm busy.

Je suis désolé, je suis occupé.
juh swee dayzolay, juh swee zokupay

Quand êtes-vous libre?
koñ et-voo leebruh
When are you free?

Say: Tuesday afternoon.

Mardi après-midi.
mardee apray meedee

C'est bon pour moi.
say boñ poor mwa
That's good for me.

Ask: What time?

A quelle heure?
ah kel ur

A quatre heures, si c'est bon pour vous.
ah katruh ur see say boñ poor voo
At four o'clock, if that's good for you.

Say: It's good for me.

C'est bon pour moi.
say boñ poor mwah

Très bien. A quelle heure?
tray byañ. ah kel ur

Okay. What time?

A trois heures, mais je suis un peu en retard.
ah trwah zur, may juh swee uñ puh oñ retar

At three o'clock, but I'm a little late.

Ne vous inquiétez pas. Asseyez-vous, je vous en prie.
nuh voo zañkyetay pah. assayay voo, juh voo zoñ pree

Don't worry. Sit down, please.

1 Warm up

Say "I'm sorry."
(pp.32–3)

What is the French for
"I'd like an
appointment"?
(pp.32–3)

How do you say "with
whom?" in French?
(pp.32–3)

Au téléphone
On the telephone

In France the emergency police
number is 17; ambulance, 15; fire, 18;
and directory assistance, 12. Phone
cards (**télécartes**) can be used for
public phones or private phones by
entering a code. They are available
from post offices
and newsstands.

2 Match and repeat

Match the numbered items to the French
in the panel on the left and test yourself.

1   **le chargeur**
    luh sharjur

2   **les renseigne-
    ments** *(m)*
    lay ronsenyumoñ

3   **le répondeur**
    luh raypoñdur

4   **le téléphone**
    luh telayfon

5   **le portable**
    luh portabluh

6   **la télécarte**
    lah telaykart

7   **les écouteurs** *(m)*
    lay zaykootur

1 charger

4 telephone

cell phone **5**

7 headphones   phone card **6**

3 In conversation

**Allô. Pauline Du Bois à
l'appareil.**
aloh. pawleen doo bwah
ah lap-paray

*Hello. Pauline du Bois
speaking.*

**Bonjour. Je voudrais
parler à Rachid
Djamal.**
boñjoor. juh voodray
parlay ah rasheed
jahmal

*Hello. I'd like to speak
to Rachid Djamal.*

**C'est de la part
de qui?**
say duh lah par duh kee

Who's calling?

4 Useful phrases

Practice these phrases. Then test yourself using the cover flap.

phone book ❷

I'd like an outside line.

Je voudrais une ligne extérieure.
juh voodray oon leenyuh exteree-yur

I'd like to speak to Françoise Martin.

Je voudrais parler à Françoise Martin.
juh voodray parlay ah franswahz martañ

❸ *answering machine*

Can I leave a message?

Je peux laisser un message?
juh puh laysay uñ mesarj

5 Say it

I'd like to speak to Mr. Hachart.

Can I leave a message for Emma?

Sorry, I have the wrong number.

Désolé(e), je me suis trompé(e) de numéro.
dayzolay, juh muh swee trompay duh noomairoe

Jean Leblanc de l'imprimerie Laporte.
joñ luhbloñ duh lahpreemuree laport

Jean Leblanc of Laporte Printers.

Désolée. La ligne est occupée.
dayzolay. lah leenyuh et okupay

I'm sorry. The line is busy.

Il peut me rappeler, s'il vous plaît?
eel puh muh raplay, seel voo play

Can he call me back, please?

Révisez et répétez
Review and repeat

1 Sums

1 seize
   sez

2 trente-neuf
   tront-nurf

3 cinquante-trois
   sankont-trwah

4 soixante-quatorze
   swasont-katorz

5 quatre-vingt dix-neuf
   katruh-vañ deeznuf

6 quarante-et-un
   karont-ay-uñ

1 Sums

Say the answers to these sums out loud in French. Then check that you have remembered correctly.

1 $10 + 6 = ?$

2 $14 + 25 = ?$

3 $66 - 13 = ?$

4 $40 + 34 = ?$

5 $90 + 9 = ?$

6 $46 - 5 = ?$

3 Telephones

What are the numbered items in French?

cell phone ❶

phone card ❸

2 I want...

1 voulez
   voolay

2 veut
   vuh

3 voulons
   vooloñ

4 veux
   vuh

5 veux
   vuh

6 veut
   vuh

2 I want...

Fill the blanks with the correct form of **vouloir**.

1 Vous _____ un café?

2 Elle _____ aller en vacances.

3 Nous _____ une table pour trois.

4 Tu _____ une bière?

5 Je _____ une nouvelle voiture.

6 Il _____ des bonbons.

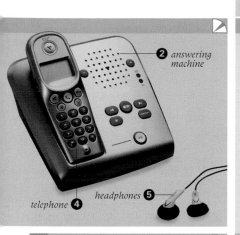

answering machine

telephone **4**   *headphones* **5**

3   Telephones

1   **le portable**
luh portabluh

2   **le répondeur**
luh raypoñdur

3   **la télécarte**
lah telaykart

4   **le téléphone**
luh telayfon

5   **les écouteurs**
lay zaykootur

4   When?

What do these sentences mean?

1   **J'ai rendez-vous lundi vingt mai.**

2   **Mon anniversaire est en septembre.**

3   **Je reviens dimanche.**

4   **Ils ne travaillent pas en août.**

4   When?

1   *I have a meeting on Monday, May 20th.*

2   *My birthday is in September.*

3   *I come back on Sunday.*

4   *They don't work in August.*

5   Time

Say these times in French.

5   Time

1   **une heure**
oon ur

2   **une heure cinq**
oon ur sank

3   **une heure vingt**
oon ur vañ

4   **une heure et demie**
oon ur ay dumee

5   **une heure et quart**
oon ur ay kar

6   **deux heures moins dix**
duh zur mwañ dees

1 Warm up

Count to 100 in tens.
(pp.10–11, pp.30–1)

Ask "At what time?"
(pp.30–1)

Say "Half-past one."
(pp.30–1)

Au guichet
At the ticket office

In France, before getting on the train, you must validate (**composter**) your ticket by stamping it. Special orange machines are installed in every train station for this purpose. Fines are handed out to those who forget to validate their tickets. Most trains have both first- and second-class seats.

2 Words to remember

Learn these words and then test yourself.

la gare lah gar	*station*
le train luh trañ	*train*
la voiture lah vwatyur	*car*
le billet luh beeyay	*ticket*
aller-simple allay-sañpluh	*one-way*
aller-retour allay-rutoor	*round-trip*
première classe prumyair klas	*first class*
en seconde oñ sugond	*second class*

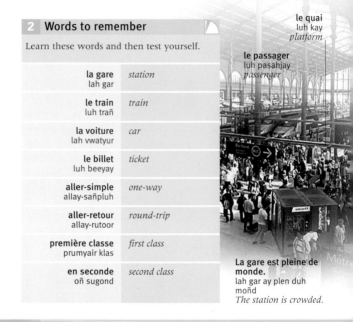

le quai
 luh kay
 platform

le passager
 luh pasahjay
 passenger

La gare est pleine de monde.
 lah gar ay plen duh moñd
 The station is crowded.

3 In conversation

Deux billets pour Bordeaux s'il vous plait.
 duh beeyay poor bordoe seel voo play

Two tickets for Bordeaux, please.

Aller-retour?
 allay rutoor

Round-trip?

Oui. Je dois réserver des places?
 wee. juh dwah rayzurvay day plas

Yes. Do I need to reserve seats?

4 Useful phrases

Learn these phrases and then test yourself using the cover flap.

How much is a ticket to Lille?	**C'est combien un billet pour Lille?** say koñbyañ uñ beeyay poor leel
Do you accept credit cards?	**Vous acceptez les cartes de crédit?** voo zakseptay lay kart duh kredee
Do I have to change trains?	**Je dois changer?** juh dwah shonjay
Which platform does the train leave from?	**Le train part de quel quai?** luh trañ par duh kel kay
Are there discounts?	**Vous faites des réductions?** voo fet day raydooksyoñ
What time does the train for Paris leave?	**A quelle heure part le train pour Paris?** ah kel ur par luh trañ poor paree

Le train pour Poitiers est annulé.
luh trañ poor pwatyer et anuley
The train to Poitiers is canceled.

5 Say it

Which platform does the train for Paris leave from?

Three tickets to Lyon, please.

🇫🇷 Cultural tip
Most train stations now have automatic ticket machines that accept credit and debit cards as well as cash.

Ce n'est pas nécessaire. Quarante euros s'il vous plaît.
suh nay pah nesaysair. karont uroh seel voo play

That's not necessary. Forty euros, please.

Vous acceptez les cartes de crédit?
voo zakseptay lay kart duh kredee

Do you accept credit cards?

Bien sûr. Le train part du quai numéro cinq.
byañ syur. luh trañ par doo kay noomairoe sank

Certainly. The train leaves from platform five.

1 Warm up

How do you say "train"? (pp.38–9)

What does "Le train part de quel quai?" mean? (pp.38–9)

Ask "When are you free?" (pp.32–3)

Aller et prendre
To go and to take

Aller (*to go*) and **prendre** (*to take*) are essential verbs in French. You can also use **prendre** to say *I'll have* (**je prends**) when you talk about food and drink. Note that the present tense in French includes the sense of a continuous action—for example, **je vais** means both *I go* and *I am going*.

2 Aller: to go

Say the different forms of **aller** (*to go*) aloud. Use the flaps to test yourself and, when you are confident, practice the sample sentences below.

je vais juh vay	*I go*
tu vas tew vah	*you go (informal singular)*
il/elle va eel/el vah	*he/she goes*
nous allons noo zalloñ	*we go*
vous allez voo zallay	*you go (formal singular or plural)*
ils/elles vont eel/el voñ	*they go*
Où allez-vous? oo allay voo	*Where are you going?*
Je vais à Paris. juh vay zah paree	*I'm going to Paris.*
Nous allons à l'école en train. noo zalloñ ah laykol oñ trañ	*We go to school by train.*

Je vais à la Tour Eiffel.
juh vay zah lah toor eefel
I'm going to the Eiffel Tower.

Cultural tip The TGV ("train à grande vitesse") is a fast train that can get you from Paris to southern France in about three hours. Generally you will need to reserve a seat and can still choose smoking or nonsmoking seats. TER ("trains express régionaux") is another type of fast train. These trains are cheaper than the TGV. You can buy a ticket on the day of travel and get on without a reservation.

3 Prendre: to take

Say the different forms of **prendre** (*to take*) aloud. Use the flaps to cover the French and test yourself. When you are confident, practice the sample sentences below.

Je prends le métro tous les jours.
juh proñ luh metroe too lay joor
I take the metro every day.

I take	**je prends** juh proñ
you take (informal singular)	**tu prends** tew proñ
he/she takes	**il/elle prend** eel/el proñ
we take	**nous prenons** noo prunoñ
you take (formal singular or plural)	**vous prenez** voo prunay
they take	**ils/elles prennent** eel/el pren

I don't want to take a taxi.	**Je ne veux pas prendre un taxi.** juh nuh vuh pah proñdruh uñ taksee
Take the first left.	**Prenez la première à gauche.** prunay lah prumyair ah gaush
He'll have the beef bourguignon.	**Il prend le bœuf bourguignon.** eel proñ luh buf boorgheenyoñ

4 Put into practice

Cover the text on the right and complete the dialogue in French.

Où allez-vous?
oo allay voo
Where are you going?

Say: *I'm going to the Louvre.*

Je vais au Louvre.
juh vay zoh loovruh

Vous voulez prendre le métro?
voo voolay proñdruh luh metroe
Do you want to take the metro?

Say: *No, I want to go by bus.*

Non, je veux aller en bus.
noñ. juh vuh allay oñ boos

Say "I'd like to go to the station." (pp.40–1)

Ask "Where are you going?" (pp.40–1)

Say "fruit" and "cheese." (pp.24–5)

Taxi, bus, et métro
Taxi, bus, and metro

With buses, as with trains, you need to validate your ticket in a machine at the time of travel. For the metro, there's a standard fare and you can also buy a **carnet**, a book of 10 tickets. It's unusual to flag down a cab in the street. You need to find one of the many taxi stands and wait there.

2   Words to remember

Familiarize yourself with these words.

le bus luh boos	*bus (local)*
le car luh kar	*bus (long-distance)*
la gare routière lah gar rootyair	*bus station*
l'arrêt de bus *(m)* laray duh boos	*bus stop*
le tarif luh tareef	*fare*
le taxi luh taksee	*taxi*
la rangée de taxis lah roñjay duh taksee	*taxi stand*
la station de métro lah stasyoñ duh metroe	*metro station*

Le bus numéro 4 s'arrête ici?
luh boos noomairoe katruh saret eesee
Does the Route 4 bus stop here?

3   In conversation: taxi

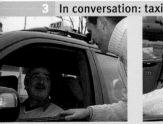

Le marché aux fromages, s'il vous plaît.
luh marshayoe fromarj, seel voo play

The cheese market, please.

Oui, sans problème, monsieur.
wee. soñ problem musyuh

Yes, no problem, sir.

Vous pouvez me déposer ici, s'il vous plaît?
voo poovay muh dayposay eesee, seel voo play

Can you drop me here, please?

4 Useful phrases

Learn these phrases and then test yourself using the cover flap.

I want a taxi to the Arc de Triomphe.	**Je veux un taxi pour l'Arc de Triomphe.** juh vuh uh taksee poor lark duh treeoñf
When is the next bus to the station?	**Quand est le prochain bus pour la gare?** koñ ay luh proshen boos poor lah gar
How do you get to the museum?	**Pour aller au musée?** poor allay oh moozay
How long is the trip?	**Le trajet dure combien de temps?** luh trajay dyur koñbyañ duh toñ
Please wait for me.	**Attendez-moi s'il vous plaît.** atonday-mwah seel voo play

█ Cultural tip Métro lines ("lignes") in Paris are known by the names of the first and last stations on the line. Follow the signs to the relevant end station—for example, direction Porte d'Orléans. Look out for the beautiful art deco "Métropolitain" signs retained in some stations.

6 Say it

Do you go near the train station?

The fruit market, please.

When's the next bus to Calais?

5 In conversation: bus

Vous allez près du musée?
vooz allay pray doo moozay

Do you go near the museum?

Oui. Ça fait quatre-vingt centimes.
wee. sah fay katruh vañ sonteem

Yes. That's 80 centimes.

Dites-moi quand on arrive, s'il vous plaît.
deet mwah koñ toñ areev, seel voo play

Tell me when we arrive, please.

1 Warm up

How do you say "I have..."? (pp.14–15)

Say "my father," "my sister," and "my parents." (pp.16–17)

Say "I'm going to Paris." (pp.40–1)

En route
On the road

Be sure to familiarize yourself with the French rules of the road before driving in France. French **autoroutes** (*highways*) are fast but expensive. They are toll (**péage**) roads in which you usually take a ticket as you enter the highway and pay according to the distance traveled as you exit.

2 Match and repeat

Match the numbered items to the list on the left, then test yourself.

1 **le coffre**
   luh kofrue

2 **le pare-brise**
   luh parbreez

3 **le capot**
   luh kapoh

4 **le pneu**
   luh pnuh

5 **la roue**
   lah roo

6 **la portière**
   lah portyair

7 **le pare-chocs**
   luh parshok

8 **les phares**
   lay far

🟦🟥 **Cultural tip** Self-service gas stations can be unstaffed. In this case, you usually have to specify how many liters you want and pay by card *before* filling up.

❶ *trunk*

❹ *tire*   ❺ *wheel*   ❻ *door*

3 Road signs

Sens unique
sons ooneek

One way

Rond-point
roñ pwañ

Roundabout

CÉDEZ LE PASSAGE

Cédez le passage
seday luh passarj

Yield

4 Useful phrases

Learn these phrases and then test yourself using the cover flap.

My turn signal doesn't work.	**Mon clignotant ne marche pas.** moñ kleenyoe-toñ nuh marsh pah
Fill it up, please.	**Le plein, s'il vous plaît.** luh plañ, seel voo play

5 Words to remember

Familiarize yourself with these words, then test yourself using the flap.

6 Say it

My gearbox doesn't work.

I have a flat tire.

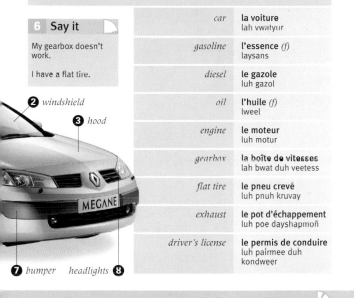

❷ *windshield*

❸ *hood*

❼ *bumper*   *headlights* ❽

MEGANE

car	**la voiture** lah vwatyur
gasoline	**l'essence** *(f)* laysans
diesel	**le gazole** luh gazol
oil	**l'huile** *(f)* lweel
engine	**le moteur** luh motur
gearbox	**la boîte de vitesses** lah bwat duh veetess
flat tire	**le pneu crevé** luh pnuh kruvay
exhaust	**le pot d'échappement** luh poe dayshapmoñ
driver's license	**le permis de conduire** luh pairmee duh kondweer

Passage protégé
passarj protayjay

Priority road

Sens interdit
sons añtairdee

Do not enter

Défense de stationner
dayfoñs duh stahseeonay

No parking

Révisez et répétez
Review and repeat

1 Transportation

1 **le bus**
luh boos

2 **le taxi**
luh taksee

3 **la voiture**
lah vwatyur

4 **le train**
luh trañ

5 **le vélo**
luh vayloe

6 **le métro**
luh metroe

1 Transportation

Name these forms of transportation in French.

bus ❶

❷ *taxi*

❹ *train*

2 Go and take

1 **allons**
alloñ

2 **vais**
vay

3 **prend**
proñ

4 **allez**
allay

5 **prenez**
prunay

6 **prends**
proñ

2 Go and take

Use the correct form of the verb in brackets.

1 Nous ____ à la Tour Eiffel. (aller)

2 Je ____ à la gare. (aller)

3 Elle ____ rendez-vous lundi. (prendre)

4 Où ____ -vous? (aller)

5 Que ____ -vous? (prendre)

6 Je ____ le bœuf. (prendre)

3 car

5 bicycle

6 metro

METROPOLITAIN

3 Vous or tu?

Use the correct form of you.

1 *You are in a café. Ask "Do you have croissants?"*

2 *You are with a friend. Ask "Do you want a beer?"*

3 *A business woman approaches you at your company reception. Ask "Do you have an appointment?"*

4 *You are on the bus. Ask "Do you go near the station?"*

5 *Ask your mother where she's going tomorrow.*

6 *Ask your client "Are you free on Wednesday?"*

3 Vous or tu?

1 **Vous avez des croissants?**
voo zavay day krossoñ

2 **Tu veux une bière?**
tew vuh oon biyair

3 **Vous avez rendez-vous?**
voo zavay roñday voo

4 **Vous allez près de la gare?**
voo zallay pray duh lah gar

5 **Où vas-tu demain?**
oo vah-tew dumañ

6 **Vous êtes libre mercredi?**
voo zet leebruh mairkrudee

4 Tickets

You're buying tickets at a train station. Follow the conversation, replying in French following the numbered English prompts.

Je peux vous aider?
1 *I'd like two tickets to Lille.*

Aller-simple ou aller-retour?
2 *Round-trip, please.*

Voilà. Cinquante euros, s'il vous plaît.
3 *What time does the train leave?*

A treize heures dix.
4 *What platform does the train leave from?*

Quai numéro sept.
5 *Thank you. Goodbye.*

4 Tickets

1 **Je voudrais deux billets pour Lille.**
juh voodray duh beeyay poor leel

2 **Aller-retour, s'il vous plaît.**
allay rutoor, seel voo play

3 **A quelle heure part le train?**
ah kel ur par luh trañ

4 **Le train part de quel quai?**
luh trañ par duh kel kay

5 **Merci. Au revoir.**
mairsee. ovwar

1 Warm up

Ask "How do you get to the musuem?"
(pp.42–3)

Say "I want to take the metro" and "I don't want to take a taxi."
(pp.40–1)

En ville
Around town

Most French towns still have a market day and a thriving community of small shops. Even small villages usually have a mayor and a town hall. There may be parking restrictions in downtwon areas. Look for signs for **parcmètres** (*pay and display*) and **défense de stationner** (*parking forbidden*).

2 Match and repeat

Match the numbered locations to the words in the panel.

1 **la mairie**
lah mayree

2 **le pont**
luh poñ

3 **le centre ville**
luh sontruh veel

4 **l'église** *(f)*
legleez

5 **le parking**
luh parking

6 **la place**
lah plas

7 **la galerie d'art**
lah galree dar

8 **le musée**
luh moozay

❹ church

❸ downtown

❶ town hall

❷ bridge

❼ art gallery

3 Words to remember

Familiarize yourself with these words and test yourself using the cover flap.

la station service la stasyoñ servees	*gas station*
le syndicat d'initiative luh sañdeekar deeneesyateev	*tourist information*
le garage luh gararj	*car repair shop*
la piscine municipale lah piseen mooneeseepal	*public swimming pool*

4 Useful phrases

Learn these phrases and then test yourself using the cover flap.

Is there an art gallery in town?	**Il y a une galerie d'art en ville?** eelyah oon galree dar oñ veel
Is it far from here?	**C'est loin d'ici?** say lwañ deesee
There is a swimming pool near the bridge.	**Il y a une piscine près du pont.** eelyah oon piseen pray doo poñ
There isn't a library.	**Il n'y a pas de bibliothèque.** eenyah pah duh bib-lee-yotek

La cathédrale est au centre-ville
lah kataydral et oh sontruh veel
The cathedral is downtown.

5 Put into practice

Join in this conversation. Read the French on the left and follow the instructions to make your reply. Then test yourself by concealing the answers with the cover flap.

❺ *parking lot*

❻ *square*

❽ *museum*

Je peux vous aider? juh puh voo zeday *Can I help you?* Ask: *Is there a library in town?*	**Il y a une bibliothèque en ville?** eelyah oon bib-lee-yotek oñ veel
Non, mais Il y a un musée. noñ may eelyah uñ moozay *No, but there's a museum.* Ask: *How do I get to the museum?*	**Pour aller au musée?** poor allay oh moozay
C'est là-bas. say lah bah *It's over there.* Say: *Thank you very much.*	**Merci beaucoup.** mairsee bohkoo

How do you say "near the station"? (pp.42–3)

Say "Take the first left." (pp.40–1)

Ask "Where are you going?" (pp.40–1)

Les directions
Finding your way

To help you find your way, you'll often find a **plan de la ville** (*town plan*) situated in the town, usually near the town hall or tourist office. In the older parts of French towns there are often narrow streets, in which you will usually find a one-way system in operation. Parking is usually restricted.

2 Useful phrases

Learn these phrases and then test yourself.

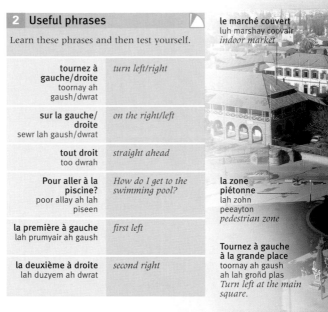

tournez à gauche/droite toornay ah gaush/dwrat	*turn left/right*
sur la gauche/droite sewr lah gaush/dwrat	*on the right/left*
tout droit too dwrah	*straight ahead*
Pour aller à la piscine? poor allay ah lah piseen	*How do I get to the swimming pool?*
la première à gauche lah prumyair ah gaush	*first left*
la deuxième à droite lah duzyem ah dwrat	*second right*

le marché couvert
luh marshay coovair
indoor market

la zone piétonne
lah zohn peeayton
pedestrian zone

Tournez à gauche à la grande place
toornay ah gaush ah lah groñd plas
Turn left at the main square.

3 In conversation

Il y a un bon restaurant en ville?
eelyah uh boñ restoroñ oñ veel

Is there a good restaurant in town?

Oui, près de la gare.
wee, pray duh lah gar

Yes, near the station.

Pour aller à la gare?
poor allay ah lah gar

How do I get to the station?

4 Words to remember

Familiarize yourself with these words and test yourself using the flap.

Je me suis perdue.
juh muh swee pairdoo
I'm lost.

traffic lights	**les feux** lay fuh	
corner	**le coin** luh kwañ	
street/road	**la rue** lah roo	
main road	**la rue principale** lah roo prañseepal	
at the end	**au bout** oh boo	
map	**la carte** lah kart	
cross	**traversez** travairsay	
across from	**en face de** oñ fass duh	

le monument
luh moonyumoñ
monument

le plan de la ville
luh plañ duh lah veel
town plan

5 Say it

Turn right at the end of the street.

It's across from the town hall.

It's ten minutes by bus.

Tournez à gauche aux feux et puis tout droit.
toornay ah gaush oh fuh ay pwee too dwrah

Turn left at the lights and then straight ahead.

C'est loin?
say lwañ

Is it far?

Non, c'est cinq minutes à pied.
noñ, say sank minoot ah pyay

No, it's five minutes on foot.

1 Warm up

Say the days of the week in French. (pp.28–9)

How do you say "at six o'clock"? (pp.30–1)

Ask "What time is it?" (pp.30–1)

Le tourisme
Sightseeing

Most national museums close on Tuesdays and public holidays. Although stores are normally closed on Sundays, in tourist areas many will remain open all weekend. It is not unusual, particularly in rural areas, for stores and public buildings to close at lunchtime.

2 Words to remember

Familiarize yourself with these words and test yourself using the flap.

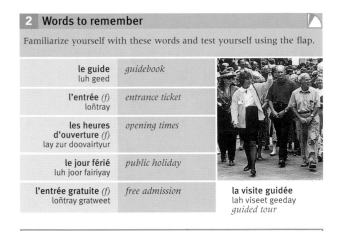

le guide luh geed	*guidebook*
l'entrée *(f)* loñtray	*entrance ticket*
les heures d'ouverture *(f)* lay zur doovairtyur	*opening times*
le jour férié luh joor fairiyay	*public holiday*
l'entrée gratuite *(f)* loñtray gratweet	*free admission*

la visite guidée
lah viseet geeday
guided tour

Cultural tip The majority of public buildings and private offices close for public holidays. Many public and private offices are closed in August. If a public holiday falls on a Thursday, the French will often *faire le pont* ("do the bridge")—in other words, take Friday off to make a long weekend.

3 In conversation

Vous ouvrez cet après-midi?
voo zoovray set apray-meedee

Do you open this afternoon?

Oui, mais nous fermons à quatre heures.
wee, may noo fairmoñ ah katruh

Yes, but we close at four o'clock.

Vous avez un accès pour les fauteuils roulants?
voo zavay uñ aksay poor lay fohtuhee roolañ

Do you have wheelchair access?

4 Useful phrases

Learn these phrases and then test yourself using the cover flap.

	What time do you open/close?	**Vous ouvrez/fermez à quelle heure?** voo zoovray/fairmay ah kel ur
	Where is the bathroom?	**Où sont les toilettes?** oo soñ lay twalet
	Is there wheelchair access?	**Il y a un accès pour les fauteuils roulants?** eelyah uñ aksay poor lay fohtuhee roolañ

5 Put into practice

Cover the text on the right and complete the dialogue in French.

Désolé. Le musée est fermé.
dezolay. luh moozay ay fairmay
Sorry. The museum is closed.

Ask: Do you open on Tuesdays?

Vous ouvrez le mardi?
voo zoovray luh mardee

Oui, mais nous fermons tôt.
wee, may noo fairmoñ toe
Yes, but we close early.

Ask: At what time?

A quelle heure?
ah kel ur

Oui, il y a un ascenseur là-bas.
wee, eelyah uñ asoñsur lah-bah

Yes, there's an elevator over there.

Merci, je voudrais quatre entrées.
mairsee, juh voodray katruh oñtray

Thank you. I'd like four admission tickets.

Voilà, et le guide est gratuit.
vwalah, ay luh geed ay gratwee

Here you are, and the guidebook is free.

1 Warm up

Say "You're on time." (pp.14–15)

What's the French for "ticket"? (pp.38–9)

Say "I am going to New York." (pp.40–1)

A l'aéroport
At the airport

Although the airport environment is largely universal, it is sometimes useful to be able to ask your way around the terminal in French. It's a good idea to make sure you have a few one-euro coins when you arrive at the airport; you may need to pay for a baggage cart.

2 Words to remember

Familiarize yourself with these words and test yourself using the flap.

l'enregistrement *(m)* loñrejeestrumoñ	*check-in*
le départ luh depar	*departures*
l'arrivée *(f)* lareevay	*arrivals*
la douane lah doo-an	*customs*
le contrôle des passeports luh kontrol day passpor	*passport control*
le terminal luh termee-nal	*terminal*
la porte d'embarquement lah port doñbarkumoñ	*gate*
le numéro de vol luh noomairoe duh vol	*flight number*

Quelle est la porte d'embarquement pour le vol numéro vingt-trois?
kel ay lah port doñbarkumoñ poor luh vol numairoh vañ-trwah
What gate does Flight 23 leave from?

3 Useful phrases

Learn these phrases and then test yourself using the cover flap.

Le vol pour Nice est à l'heure? luh vol poor nees et ah lur	*Is the flight to Nice on time?*
Je ne trouve pas mes bagages. juh nuh troov pah may bagarj	*I can't find my baggage.*
Le vol pour Londres est retardé. luh vol poor londruh ay retarday	*The flight to London is delayed.*

4 Put into practice

Join in this conversation. Read the French on the left and follow the instructions to make your reply. Then test yourself by concealing the answers with the cover flap.

Bonsoir, monsieur. Je peux vous aider?
boñswar, musyuh. juh puh voo zayday
Good evening, sir. Can I help you?

Ask: Is the flight to Paris on time?

Le vol pour Paris est à l'heure?
luh vol poor paree et ah lur

Oui, monsieur
wee musyuh
Yes, sir.

Ask: What gate does it leave from?

Quelle est la porte d'embarquement?
kel ay lah port doñbarkumoñ

5 Match and repeat

Match the numbered items to the French words in the panel.

boarding pass ➊

baggage ➋ check-in

ticket ➌

passport ➍

➎ suitcase   ➏ carry-on luggage   ➐ cart

1 **la carte d'embarquement**
lah kart doñbarkumoñ

2 **l'enregistrement des bagages** *(m)*
loñrejeestrumoñ day bagarj

3 **le billet**
luh beeyay

4 **le passeport**
luh passpor

5 **la valise**
lah valeez

6 **le bagage à main**
luh bagarj ah mañ

7 **le chariot**
luh shareeyoh

Révisez et répétez
Review and repeat

1 Places

1 **le musée**
luh moozay

2 **la mairie**
lah mayree

3 **le pont**
luh poñ

4 **la galerie d'art**
lah galree dar

5 **le parking**
luh parking

6 **la cathédrale**
lah kataydral

7 **la place**
lah plas

1 Places

Name the numbered places in French.

❶ *museum*   ❷ *town hall*   ❸ *bridge*

❹ *art gallery*   ❺ *parking lot*

❻ *cathedral*

❼ *square*

2 Car parts

1 **le pare-brise**
luh parbreez

2 **le clignotant**
luh kleenyoe-toñ

3 **le capot**
luh kapoh

4 **le pneu**
luh pnuh

5 **la portière**
lah portyair

6 **le pare-chocs**
luh parshok

2 Car parts

Name these car parts in French.

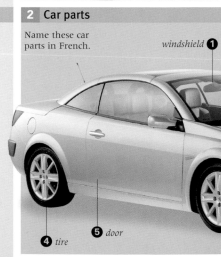

windshield ❶

❹ *tire*   ❺ *door*

3 Questions

Ask the questions that match these answers.

1 **Le car part à huit heures.**
luh kar par ah weet ur

2 **Le café, c'est deux euros cinquante.**
luh kafay, say duh zuroh sankont

3 **Non, je ne veux pas de vin.**
noñ. juh nuh vuh pah duh vañ

4 **Le train part du quai cinq.**
luh trañ par doo kay sank

5 **Nous allons à Paris.**
noo zalloñ ah paree

6 **Non, c'est cinq minutes à pied.**
noñ, say sank minoot ah pyay

3 Questions

1 **Le car part à quelle heure?**
luh kar par ah kel ur

2 **C'est combien le café?**
say koñbyañ luh kafay

3 **Vous voulez du vin?**
voo voolay doo vañ

4 **Le train part de quel quai?**
luh trañ par duh kel kay

5 **Où allez-vous?**
oo allay voo

6 **C'est loin?**
say lwañ

② *turn signal*
③ *hood*
⑥ *bumper*

MEGANE

4 Verbs

Choose the correct words to fill the gaps.

1 Je _____ anglais.

2 Nous _____ le bus.

3 Elle _____ à Paris.

4 Il _____ trois filles.

5 Tu _____ un thé?

6 Combien d'enfants _____ -vous?

7 Je _____ rendez-vous pour mardi.

8 Où _____ les toilettes?

4 Verbs

1 **suis**
swee

2 **prenons**
prunoñ

3 **va**
vah

4 **a**
ah

5 **veux**
vuh

6 **avez**
avay

7 **prends**
proñ

8 **sont**
soñ

1 Warm up

How do you ask in French "Do you accept credit cards?" (pp.38–9)

Ask "How much is that?" (pp.18–19)

Ask "Do you have children?" (pp.12–13)

Réserver les chambres
Booking a room

There are different types of accommodation: **l'hôtel**, categorized from one to five stars; **la pension**, a small family-run hotel; and **les chambres d'hôte** (like bed and breakfast) which are often situated in beautiful old properties.

2 Useful phrases

Practice these phrases and then test yourself by concealing the French on the left with the cover flap.

Le petit-déjeuner est compris? luh puhtee dayjunay ay koñpree	*Is breakfast included?*
Vous acceptez les animaux de compagnie? voo zakseptay lay zanimoe duh koñpañee	*Do you accept pets?*
Vous avez un room service? voo zavay uñ room survees	*Do you have room service?*
Il faut libérer la chambre à quelle heure? eel foe leeburay lah shombruh ah kel ur	*What time do I have to check out?*

3 In conversation

Vous avez des chambres libres?
voo zavay day shombruh leebruh

Do you have any vacancies?

Oui, une chambre double.
wee, oon shombruh doobluh

Yes, a double room.

Vous avez un lit d'enfant?
voo zavay uñ lee doñfoñ

Do you have a crib?

4 Words to remember

Familiarize yourself with these words and test yourself by concealing the French on the right with the cover flap.

La chambre donne sur le jardin?
lah shombruh don syur luh jardañ
Does the room have a view over the garden?

room	**la chambre**	lah shombruh
single room	**la chambre simple**	lah shombruh sampluh
double room	**la chambre double**	lah shombruh doobluh
twin room	**la chambre twin**	lah shombruh twin
bathroom	**la salle de bains**	lah sal duh bañ
shower	**la douche**	lah doosh
breakfast	**le petit-déjeuner**	luh puhtee dayjunay
key	**la clé**	lah klay
balcony	**le balcon**	luh balkoñ
air-conditioning	**la climatisation**	lah kleematee-zasyoñ

5 Say it

Do you have a single room?

Does the room have a balcony?

Cultural tip "Chambres d'hôte" are usually the only type of accommodation to include breakfast in the price of the room. In other types of hotels, you will usually be charged extra. Many two- or three-star hotels belong to the Logis de France association, which guarantees certain standards of accommodation and service.

Pas de problème. Combien de nuits?
pah duh prob-lem. koñbyañ duh nwee

No problem. How many nights?

Pour trois nuits.
poor trwah nwee

For three nights

Très bien. Voici la clé.
tray byañ. vwasee lah klay

Very good. Here's the key.

1 Warm up

How do you say "is there...?" and "there isn't..."? (pp.48–9)

What does "Je peux vous aider?" mean? (pp.48–9)

A l'hôtel
In the hotel

Although the larger hotels almost always have private bathrooms, there are still some **pensions** and **chambres d'hôte** with shared facilities. This can also be the case in some economy hotels, where a whole family can stay overnight for less than the price of a tank of gas.

2 Match and repeat

Match the numbered items in this hotel bedroom with the French text in the panel and test yourself using the cover flap.

1 **la table de chevet**
lah tabluh duh shuvay

2 **la lampe**
lah lomp

3 **la stéréo**
lah stairayoe

4 **les rideaux** *(m)*
lay reedoe

5 **le canapé**
luh kanapay

6 **l'oreiller** *(m)*
lorayay

7 **le coussin**
luh koosañ

8 **le lit**
luh lee

9 **le dessus de lit**
luh dusoo duh lee

10 **la couverture**
lah coovurtyur

❶ *nightstand*
❷ *lamp*
❸ *stereo system*
❹ *curtains*
sofa ❺
❻ *pillow*
❼ *cushion*
❽ *bed*
❾ *bedspread*
blanket ❿

🔲🔲 **Cultural tip** When you arrive in your room, you will usually see a long sausage-shaped pillow on the bed called "le traversin"—nowadays a largely decorative item. These are hard and not very comfortable. However, you can usually find square, softer pillows ("les oreillers") in the cupboard. Do not hesitate to ask if you can't find any.

3 Useful phrases

Familiarize yourself with these phrases and then test yourself.

The room is too cold/hot.	**La chambre est trop froide/chaude.** lah shombruh ay troe fwrard/shohd
There are no towels.	**Il n'y a pas de serviettes.** eenyah pah duh survyet
I need some soap.	**J'ai besoin de savon.** jay buzwañ duh savoñ
The shower doesn't work very well.	**La douche ne marche pas très bien.** lah doosh nuh marsh pah tray byañ
The elevator has broken down.	**L'ascenseur est en panne.** lasohsur ay toñ pan

4 Put into practice

Cover the text on the right and complete the dialogue in French.

Je peux vous aider? juh puh voo zayday *Can I help you?*

Say: I need some pillows.

J'ai besoin d'oreillers. jay buzwañ dorayay

La femme de chambre va les apporter. la fam duh shambruh vah lay zaportay *The maid will bring some.*

Say: And the television doesn't work.

Et la télévision ne marche pas. ay lah telayveesyoñ nuh marsh pah

1 Warm up

Ask "Can I?" (pp.34–5)

What is French for "the shower"? (pp.60–1)

Say "I need some towels." (pp.60–1)

Au camping
At the campground

Camping is popular in France and there are many well-organized campgrounds. These are rated by a star system. Most towns have **un camping municipal** (*public campground*), and there are also many private sites. Campfires are usually forbidden, but you can often rent a barbecue grill.

2 Useful phrases

Familiarize yourself with these phrases and then test yourself using the cover flap.

Je peux louer un vélo?
juh puh looway uñ vayloe
Can I rent a bicycle?

C'est de l'eau potable?
say duh loe potabluh
Is this drinking water?

Les feux de camp sont permis?
lay fuh duh koñ soñ pairmee
Are campfires allowed?

Les radios sont interdites.
lay radyo soñ añtairdeet
Radios are forbidden.

le double toit
luh doobluh twah
fly sheet

Le camping est tranquille
luh komping ay troñkeel
The campground is quiet.

le bureau du camping
luh buroh doo komping
campground office

la poubelle
lah poobel
trash can

3 In conversation

J'ai besoin d'un emplacement pour trois nuits.
jay buzwañ d'uñ oñplasmoñ poor trwah nwee

I need a site for three nights.

Il y en a un près de la piscine.
eelyon ah uñ pray duh lah piseen

There's one near the swimming pool.

C'est combien pour une caravane?
say koñbyañ poor oon karavan

How much is it for a camper?

4 Words to remember

Familiarize yourself with these words and test yourself using the flap.

5 Say it

I need a site for four nights.

Can I rent a tent?

Where's the electrical hookup?

les toilettes (f)
lay twalet
restrooms

le branchement électrique
luh bronshmoñ aylektreek
electrical hookup

la corde
lah kord
guy rope

le piquet
luh peekay
tent peg

tent	**la tente** lah tont
camper trailer	**la caravane** lah karavan
camper van	**le camping-car** luh komping-car
campground	**le camping** luh komping
site	**l'emplacement** (m) loñplasmoñ
campfire	**le feu de camp** luh fuh duh koñ
drinking water	**l'eau potable** (f) loe potabluh
garbage	**les détritus** (m) lay daytreetoo
showers	**les douches** (f) lay doosh
stove fuel	**le camping-gaz** luh komping-gaz
sleeping bag	**le sac de couchage** luh sak duh koosharj
air mattress	**le matelas pneumatique** luh mataylah nyumateek
groundsheet	**le tapis de sol** luh tapee duh sol

Cinquante euros, avec une nuit d'avance.
sankoñt uroh, avek oon nwee davons

Fifty euros, one night in advance.

Je peux louer un barbecue?
juh puh looway uñ barbekyoo

Can I rent a barbecue grill?

Oui, mais vous devez verser des arrhes.
wee, may voo duvay vairsay day zar

Yes, but you must pay a deposit.

1 Warm up

Say "hot" and "cold."
(pp.60–1)

What is the French
for "bathroom"
(pp.58–9), "bed," and
"pillow"? (pp.60–1)

Les descriptions
Descriptions

Adjectives are words used to describe
people, things, and places. In French
you generally put the adjective after
the thing it describes—for example,
une chambre froide (*a cold room*), but
in some cases the adjective is placed
before—for example, **un grand café**
(*a large coffee*).

2 Words to remember

Adjectives can change slightly depending on whether the thing
described is masculine (**le**), feminine (**la**), or plural (**les**), but often
this affects only the spelling, not the pronunciation. Below, the
masculine spelling is followed by the feminine. For the plural form,
just add a (silent) "s" to the appropriate masculine or feminine form.

grand/grande groñ/groñd	*big/tall*
petit/petite puhtee/puhteet	*small*
chaud/chaude shoh/shohd	*hot*
froid/froide fwrah/fwrad	*cold*
bon/bonne boñ/bon	*good*
mauvais/mauvaise movay/movez	*bad*
lent/lente loñ/lont	*slow*
rapide/rapide rapeed/rapeed	*fast*
bruyant/bruyante breeyoñ/breeyont	*noisy*
tranquille/tranquille troñkeel/troñkeel	*quiet*
dur/dure dyuh/dyuh	*hard*
mou/molle moo/moll	*soft*
beau/belle boe/bell	*beautiful*
laid/laide leh/led	*ugly*

la haute montagne
lah oht moñtanhyuh
high mountain

la petite maison
lah puhteet mayzon
small house

la vieille église
lah veeyay egleez
old church

la basse colline
lah bas koleen
low hill

**Le village est très
beau.**
luh veelarj ay tray boe
*The village is very
beautiful.*

3 Useful phrases

You can emphasize a description by using **très** (*very*), **trop** (*too*), or **plus** (*more*) before the adjective.

This coffee is cold.	**Ce café est froid.** suh kafay ay fwrah
My room is very noisy.	**Ma chambre est très bruyante.** mah shombruh ay tray breeyont
My car is too small.	**Ma voiture est trop petite.** mah vwatyur ay troe puhteet
I need a softer bed.	**J'ai besoin d'un lit plus mou.** jay buzwañ d'uñ lee ploo moo

4 Put into practice

Join in this conversation. Cover up the text on the right and complete the dialogue in French. Check and repeat if necessary.

Voici la chambre.
vwasee lah shombruh
Here is the bedroom.

Say: *The view is very beautiful.*

La vue est très belle.
lah voo ay tray bell

La salle de bains est là-bas.
luh sal duh bañ ay lah-bah
The bathroom is over there.

Say: *It is too small.*

Elle est trop petite.
el ay troe puhteet

Nous n'en avons pas d'autre.
noo nañavoñ pah dotruh
We don't have another one.

Say: *Then we'll take the room.*

Alors nous prenons la chambre.
Alor noo prunoñ lah shombruh

Révisez et répétez
Review and repeat

1 Adjectives

1 Adjectives

Put the adjective in brackets into French, using the correct masculine or feminine form.

1 La chambre est trop _____ . (hot)

2 Je voudrais un oreiller plus _____ . (soft)

3 Le café est _____ . (good)

4 Cette salle de bains est trop _____ . (small)

5 Vous avez une chambre plus _____ ? (quiet)

Answers (column):

1 **chaude**
shohd

2 **mou**
moo

3 **bon**
boñ

4 **petite**
puhteet

5 **tranquille**
troñkeel

2 Campground

2 Campground

Name these items you might find in a campground.

1 electrical hookup
2 tent
3 trash can
4 guy rope

Answers (column):

1 **le branchement électrique**
luh bronshmoñ aylektreek

2 **la tente**
lah tont

3 **la poubelle**
lah poobel

4 **la corde**
lah kord

5 **les toilettes**
lay twalet

6 **la caravane**
lah karavan

3 At the hotel

You are booking a room in a hotel. Follow the conversation, replying in French following the English prompts.

Je peux vous aider?
1 *Do you have any vacancies?*

Oui, une chambre double.
2 *Do you accept pets?*

Oui. C'est pour combien de nuits?
3 *Three nights.*

Ça fait deux cent quarante euros.
4 *Is breakfast included?*

Bien sûr, voici la clé.
5 *Thank you very much.*

3 At the hotel

1 **Vous avez des chambres libres?**
voo zavay day shombruh leebruh

2 **Vous acceptez les animaux de compagnie?**
voo zakseptay lay zanimoe duh koñpañee

3 **Trois nuits.**
trwah nwee

4 **Le petit-déjeuner est compris?**
luh puhtee dayjuhnay ay koñpree

5 **Merci beaucoup.**
mairsee bohkoo

---

5 *bathrooms*

6 *camper*

4 Negatives

Make these sentences negative using the verb in brackets.

1 Je ___ d'enfants. (avoir)

2 Elle ___ à Paris demain. (aller)

3 Il ___ de vin. (vouloir)

4 Je ___ le train pour Nice. (prendre)

5 Le café ___ chaud. (être)

4 Negatives

1 **n'ai pas**
nay pah

2 **ne va pas**
nuh vah pah

3 **ne veut pas**
nuh vuh pah

4 **ne prends pas**
nuh proñ pah

5 **n'est pas**
nay pah

1 Warm up

Ask "How do I get to the station?" (pp.50–1)

Say "Turn left at the traffic lights"; "Cross the street"; "The station is across from the café." (pp.50–1)

Les magasins
Stores

In downtown areas, stores (**magasins**) are often traditional specialty shops. But you can also find big supermarkets and shopping malls on the outskirts of major towns. Local markets selling fresh, local produce can be found everywhere. You can find out which day is market day at the tourist office.

2 Match and repeat

Match the numbered shops below and right to the French in the panel. Then test yourself using the cover flap.

1 **la boulangerie**
lah booloñjuree

2 **la pâtisserie**
lah pateesree

3 **le tabac**
luh tabah

4 **la boucherie**
lah boosheree

5 **la charcuterie**
lah sharkooterie

6 **la librairie**
lah leebrairee

7 **la poissonnerie**
lah pwasoñree

8 **l'épicerie** *(m)*
laypeesree

9 **la banque**
lah boñk

❶ *bread shop*

❷ *bakery*

❹ *butcher shop*

❺ *delicatessen*

❼ *fishmonger*

❽ *grocery store*

▐▐ Cultural tip As well as supplying medicines and health products, a French pharmacy ("pharmacie") will sell expensive perfume and cosmetics but not generally an everyday bar of soap or a tube of toothpaste. The latter are found at the supermarket or general store. The "tabac" (tobacconist) is the place for newspapers and stamps, but also often incorporates a café and bar.

3 Words to remember

Familiarize yourself with these words and test yourself using the flap.

Où est la fleuriste?
oo ay lah flureest
Where is the florist?

❸ *tobacconist*

❻ *bookstore*

❾ *bank*

hardware store	**la quincaillerie** lah kañkayeree
antique shop	**l'antiquaire** *(m)* lañteekair
hairdresser	**le coiffeur** luh kwafur
jeweler	**la bijouterie** lah bee-jooteree
post office	**la poste** lah post
shoemaker	**la cordonnerie** lah kordoneree
dry-cleaner	**le pressing** luh praysing
candy store	**le confiseur** luh koñfeesur
cheese shop	**la fromagerie** lah fromajeree

4 Useful phrases

Familiarize yourself with these phrases.

Where is the hairdresser?	**Où est le coiffeur?** oo ay luh kwafur
Where do I pay?	**Je dois payer où?** juh dwah payay oo
I'm just looking, thank you.	**Je regarde, merci.** juh rugard, mairsee
Do you sell phone cards?	**Vous vendez des télécartes?** voo vonday day telaykart
I'd like two of these.	**J'en veux deux.** joñ vuh duh
Is there a department store in town?	**Il y a un grand magasin en ville?** eelyah uñ groñ magazañ oñ veel
Can I place an order?	**Je peux passer une commande?** juh puh passay oon komond

5 Say it

Where is the bank?

Do you sell cheese?

Where do I pay?

1 Warm up

What is French for 40, 56, 77, 82, and 94? (pp.30–1)

Say "I'd like a big room." (pp.64–5)

Ask "Do you have a small car?" (pp.64–5)

Au marché
At the market

France uses the metric system of weights and measures. You need to ask for produce in kilograms or grams. You may find that the older generation still uses the term **une livre** (*a pound*) meaning half a kilogram. Some larger items such as melons are sold individually—**à la pièce**.

2 Match and repeat

Match the numbered items in this scene with the text in the panel.

1 **les courgettes** *(f)*
   lay korjet

2 **la salade**
   lah sah-lad

3 **les citrons** *(m)*
   lay sitroñ

4 **les poireaux** *(m)*
   lay pwaroe

5 **les tomates** *(f)*
   lay toemat

6 **les champignons** *(m)*
   lay shoñpeeyoñ

7 **les avocats** *(m)*
   lay zavokah

8 **les pommes de terre** *(f)*
   lay pom duh tair

❶ *zucchini*

tomatoes ❺   ❽ *potatoes*

mushrooms ❻   ❼ *avocados*

3 In conversation

Je voudrais des tomates.
juh voodray day toemat

I'd like some tomatoes.

Des grosses ou des petites?
day gros oo day puhteet

The large ones or the small ones?

Deux kilos de grosse, s'il vous plaît.
duh keeloe duh gros, seel voo play

Two kilos of the large ones, please.

🇫🇷 **Cultural tip** France now uses the common European currency, the euro. This is divided into 100 cents, which the French call "centimes" after the old divisions of the franc. You will usually hear the price given as: dix euros, vingt (€10.20), six euros, soixante-treize (€6.73), etc.

❷ *lettuce*

❸ *lemons*

❹ *leeks*

4 Useful phrases

Learn these phrases. Then cover up the answers on the right. Read the English under the pictures and say the phrase in French as shown on the right.

The goat's cheese is too expensive.

Le fromage de chèvre est trop cher.
luh fromarj duh shevruh ay troe shair

How much is that cheese?

C'est combien ce fromage?
say koñbyañ suh fromarj

5 Say it

Three kilos of potatoes, please.

The mushrooms are too expensive.

How much is the lettuce?

That's all.

Ce sera tout.
suh surah too

Et avec ceci, madame.
ay avek susee, ma-dam

Anything else, madam?

**Ce sera tout, merci.
C'est combien?**
suh surah too, mairsee.
say koñbyañ

*That's all, thank you.
How much?*

Trois euros, cinquante.
trwah zuroh, sankont

Three euros fifty.

Au supermarché
At the supermarket

Prices in supermarkets are usually
lower than in small shops. They offer
all kinds of products, with larger out-
of-town **hypermarchés** (*hypermarkets*)
extending to clothes, household
goods, garden furniture, and home-
improvement products. They may
also stock regional products.

2 Match and repeat

Look at the numbered items and match them to the French words in
the panel on the left.

1 **les produits
d'entretien** *(m)*
lay prodwee
doñtruh-tiañ

2 **les fruits** *(m)*
lay froo-wee

3 **les boissons** *(m)*
lay bwassoñ

4 **les plats
préparés** *(m)*
lay plah prayparay

5 **les légumes** *(m)*
lay laygoom

6 **les produits
surgelés** *(m)*
lay prodwee
surjulay

7 **les produits
laitiers** *(m)*
lay prodwee letyay

8 **les produits de
beauté** *(m)*
lay prodwee duh
boetay

household products **1**

fruit **2**

drinks **3**

*prepared
meals* **4**

vegetables **5**

frozen foods **6**

Cultural tip Fruit and vegetables sold by the
kilo are usually weighed and priced at a separate counter.
Alternatively, there may sometimes be a self-service
weighing machine.

3 Useful phrases

Learn these phrases and then test yourself using the cover flap.

	May I have a bag, please?	**Je peux avoir un sac, s'il vous plaît?** juh puh avwar uñ sak, seel voo play
	Where is the drinks aisle?	**Où est le rayon des boissons?** oo ay luh rayonn day bwassoñ
	Where is the checkout, please?	**Où est la caisse, s'il vous plaît?** oo ay lah kes, seel voo play
	Please type in your PIN.	**Tapez votre code, s'il vous plaît.** tapay votruh kod, seel voo play

4 Words to remember

Learn these words and then test yourself using the cover flap.

8 *beauty products*

7 *dairy products*

bread	**le pain** luh pañ
milk	**le lait** luh lay
butter	**le beurre** luh bur
ham	**le jambon** luh joñboñ
salt	**le sel** luh sel
pepper	**le poivre** luh pwavruh
laundry detergent	**la lessive** lah leseev
toilet paper	**le papier toilette** luh papyay twalet
diapers	**les couches** *(f)* lay koosh
dishwashing liquid	**le liquide vaisselle** luh likeed vaysel

5 Say it

Where's the dairy products aisle?

May I have some ham, please?

Where are the frozen foods?

1 Warm up

Say "I'd like...."
(pp.22–3)

Ask "Do you have...?
(pp.14–15)

Say "38," "42," and
"46." (pp.30–1)

Say "large," "small,"
"bigger," and
"smaller." (pp.64–5)

Vêtements et chaussures
Clothes and shoes

Clothes and shoes are measured in metric sizes. Even allowing for conversion of sizes, French clothes tend to be cut smaller than American ones. Note that clothes size is **la taille** but shoe size is **la pointure**.

2 Match and repeat

Match the numbered items of clothing to the French words in the panel on the left. Use the cover flap to test yourself.

1 **la chemise**
lah shumeez

2 **la cravate**
lah kravat

3 **la veste**
lah vest

4 **la poche**
lah posh

5 **la manche**
lah moñsh

6 **le pantalon**
luh poñtaloñ

7 **la jupe**
lah joop

8 **le collants** *(m)*
luh kolloñ

9 **les chaussures** *(f)*
lay shohsyur

shirt **1**

tie **2**

jacket **3**

pocket **4**

sleeve **5**

pants **6**

Cultural tip Like most of Europe, France uses the continental system of clothing sizes. Dress sizes usually range from 36 (US 6) through to 46 (US 18) and shoe sizes from 37 (US 6) to 45 (US 12). For men's shirts, a size 41 is a 16-inch collar, 43 is a 17-inch collar, and 45 is an 18-inch collar.

3 Useful phrases

Learn these phrases and then test yourself using the cover flap.

Do you have a larger size?

Vous avez une taille plus grande?
voo zavay oon tie ploo groñd

It's not what I want.

Ce n'est pas ce que je veux.
suh nay pah sukuh juh vuh

I'll take the pink one.

Je prends la rose.
juh proñ lah roz

4 Words to remember

Colors are adjectives (pp.64–5) and often have a masculine, feminine, and plural form. The feminine is usually formed by adding an "e" and the plural by adding an "s."

red	**rouge/rouge** rooj/rooj
white	**blanc/blanche** bloñ/blonsh
blue	**bleu/bleue** bluh/bluh
yellow	**jaune/jaune** jon/jon
green	**vert/verte** vair/vairt
black	**noir/noire** nwar/nwar

7 *skirt*

8 *pantyhose*

9 *shoes*

5 Say it

I'll take the yellow one.

Do you have this jacket in black?

I'd like a 38.

Do you have a smaller size?

Révisez et répétez
Review and repeat

Réponses
Answers
Cover with flap

1 Market

1 **les tomates**
lay toemat

2 **les champignons**
lay shoñpeeyoñ

3 **les pommes de terre**
lay pom duh tair

4 **les courgettes**
lay korjet

5 **la salade**
lah sah-lad

6 **les avocats**
lay zavokah

1 Market

Name the numbered vegetables in French.

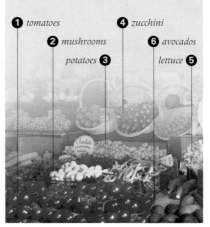

1 *tomatoes*
2 *mushrooms*
potatoes 3
4 *zucchini*
6 *avocados*
lettuce 5

2 Description

1 *These shoes are too expensive.*

2 *My room is very small.*

3 *I need a softer bed.*

2 Description

What do these sentences mean?

1 **Ces chaussures sont trop chères.**

2 **Ma chambre est très petite.**

3 **J'ai besoin d'un lit plus mou.**

3 Shops

1 **la boulangerie**
lah booloñjuree

2 **l'épicerie**
laypeesree

3 **la librairie**
lah leebrairee

4 **la poissonnerie**
lah pwasoñree

5 **la pâtisserie**
lah pateesree

6 **la boucherie**
lah boosheree

3 Shops

Name the numbered shops in French, then check your answers.

1 *bread shop* 2 *grocery* 3 *bookshop*

4 *fishmonger* 5 *bakery* 6 *butcher*

4 Supermarket

What is the French for the numbered product categories?

❶ *household products*

❷ *beauty products*

❸ *drinks*

❹ *dairy products*

❺ *frozen foods*

4 Supermarket

1 **les produits d'entretien**
lay prodwee doñtruh-tiañ

2 **les produits de beauté**
lay prodwee duh boetay

3 **les boissons**
lay bwassoñ

4 **les produits laitiers**
lay prodwee letyay

5 **les produits surgelés**
lay prodwee surjulay

5 Museum

Follow this conversation replying in French following the English prompts.

Bonjour. Je peux vous aider?
1 *Three adults and two children.*

Ça fait soixante-dix euros.
2 *That's very expensive!*

Nous ne faisons pas de réductions pour les enfants.
3 *How much is a guide?*

Quinze euros.
4 *Five tickets and a guide, please.*

Quatre-vingt-cinq euros, s'il vous plaît.
5 *Here you are. Where are the restrooms?*

Là-bas.
6 *Thank you very much.*

5 Museum

1 **Trois adultes et deux enfants.**
trwah zadoolt ay duh zoñfoñ

2 **C'est très cher!**
say tray shair

3 **C'est combien pour un guide?**
say koñbyañ poor uñ geed

4 **Cinq entrées et un guide, s'il vous plaît**
sank oñtray ay tuñ geed, seel voo play

5 **Voilà. Où sont les toilettes?**
vwalah, oo soñ lay twalet

6 **Merci beaucoup.**
mairsee bohkoo

1 Warm up

Ask "which platform?" (pp.38–9)

What is the French for the following family members: "sister," "brother," "mother," "father," "son," and "daughter"? (pp.10–11)

Occupations
Jobs

Some occupations have a different form when the person is female—for example, **infirmier** (*male nurse*) and **infirmière** (*female nurse*). Others, such as **professeur**, remain the same for men and women. When you say your occupation, you don't use **un/une** (*a*), as in **Je suis avocat** (*I'm a lawyer*).

2 Words to remember: jobs

Familiarize yourself with these occupations and test yourself using the flap. The feminine form is shown in parentheses.

médecin medsañ	*doctor*
dentiste doñteest	*dentist*
infirmier(ière) añfairmyay(yair)	*nurse*
professeur profesur	*teacher*
comptable koñtabluh	*accountant*
avocat(e) avokah(aht)	*lawyer*
designer deesienur	*designer*
consultant(e) koñsooltoñ(oñt)	*consultant*
secrétaire sekraytair	*secretary*
commerçant(e) komairsoñ(oñt)	*shopkeeper*
électricien(ne) aylektreesyañ(en)	*electrician*
plombier ploñbyay	*plumber*
cuisinier(ière) kweeseenyay(yair)	*cook/chef*
ingénieur añjaynyur	*engineer*
à mon compte ah moñ kont	*self-employed*

Je suis plombier.
juh swee ploñbyay
I'm a plumber.

Elle est professeur.
el ay profesur
She is a teacher.

3 Put into practice

Join in the conversation. Conceal the text on the right with the cover flap and complete the dialogue in French.

Quelle est votre profession?
kel ay votruh profesyoñ
What do you do?

Say: I am a consultant.

Je suis consultant.
juh swee koñsooltoñ

Vous travaillez pour quelle compagnie?
voo trav-eyeyay poor kel koñpanee
What company do you work for?

Say: I'm self-employed.

Je suis à mon compte.
juh swee ah moñ kont

Comme c'est intéressant!
kom say añtayraysoñ
How interesting!

Ask: What is your profession?

Et quelle est votre profession?
ay kel ay votruh profesyoñ

Je suis dentiste.
juh swee doñteest
I'm a dentist.

Say: My sister is a dentist, too.

Ma sœur est dentiste aussi.
mah sur ay doñteest ohsee

4 Words to remember: workplace

Familiarize yourself with these words and test yourself.

headquarters	**le siège social** luh syej sosyal	
branch	**lah succursale** lah sookoorsal	
department	**le département** luh daypartumoñ	
reception	**la réception** lah resepsyoñ	
manager	**le chef** luh shef	
trainee	**le stagiaire** luh stajyair	

Le siège social est à Lille.
luh syej sosyal ay tah leel
Headquarters is in Lille.

Practice different ways of introducing yourself in different situations (pp.8–9). Mention your name, occupation, nationality, and any other information you'd like to volunteer.

Le bureau
The office

An office environment or business situation has its own vocabulary in any language, but there are many items for which the terminology is virtually universal. Be aware that French computer keyboards have a different layout from the standard English "QWERTY" convention.

2 Words to remember

Familiarize yourself with these words. Read them aloud several times and try to memorize them. Conceal the French with the cover flap and test yourself.

le moniteur luh moneetur	*monitor*
l'ordinateur *(m)* lordeenatur	*computer*
la souris lah sooree	*mouse*
l'email *(m)* leemail	*email*
l'internet *(m)* lañtairnet	*Internet*
le mot de passe luh moh duh pas	*password*
la messagerie téléphonique lah mesah-juree telayfoneek	*voicemail*
le fax luh fax	*fax machine*
le copieur luh kopee-ur	*photocopier*
l'agenda *(m)* lajeñdah	*planner*
la carte de visite lah kart duh veezeet	*business card*
la réunion lah rayoonyon	*meeting*
la conférence lah konfayroñs	*conference*
l'ordre du jour *(m)* lordruh doo joor	*agenda*

❶ *lamp*

screen **❹**

❷ *stapler*

telephone **❸**

pen **❿**

notepad **⓫**

drawer **⓬**

3 Useful phrases

Learn these phrases and then test yourself using the cover flap.

I need to make some photocopies.	**J'ai besoin de faire des photocopies.** jay buzwañ duh fair day fotokopee
I'd like to arrange an appointment.	**Je voudrais prendre rendez-vous.** juh voodray proñdruh roñday-voo
I want to send an email.	**Je veux envoyer un email.** juh vuh oñvwayay uñ eemail

4 Match and repeat

Match the numbered items to the French words on the right.

5 *keyboard*

6 *laptop*

printer **9**

7 *desk*

8 *clock*

13 *swivel chair*

1 **la lampe**
lah lomp

2 **l'agrafeuse** *(f)*
lagrafurz

3 **le téléphone**
luh telayfon

4 **l'écran** *(m)*
laykroñ

5 **le clavier**
luh klaveeyay

6 **l'ordinateur portable** *(m)*
lordeenatur portabluh

7 **le bureau**
luh byuroh

8 **la pendule**
lah poñdool

9 **l'imprimante** *(f)*
lampreemont

10 **le stylo**
luh steeloh

11 **le bloc-notes**
luh blok-not

12 **le tiroir**
luh teerwar

13 **la chaise tournante**
lah shayz toornont

5 Say it

I'd like to arrange a conference.

I need to send a fax.

Do you have a laptop?

1 Warm up

Say "How interesting!" (p.78–9), "library" (pp.48–9), and "traffic lights." (pp.50–1)

Ask "What is your profession?" and answer "I'm an engineer." (pp.78–9)

Le monde académique
Academic world

In France, **une licence** (*bachelor's degree*) generally takes three years, followed by **une maîtrise** (*master's degree*) and **un doctorat** (*Ph.D.*). Paris has several universities, often referred to by Roman numerals, as in Paris V.

2 Useful phrases

Familiarize yourself with these phrases and then test yourself.

Quel est votre secteur? kel ay votruh sektur	*What is your field?*
Je fais de la recherche en chimie. juh fay duh lah reshairsh oñ sheemee	*I am doing research in chemistry.*
J'ai une licence en droit. jay oon leesons oñ dwrah	*I have a degree in law.*
Je fais une présentation sur l'architecture moderne. juh fay oon praysoñtasyoñ syur larsheetektur modairn	*I am giving a presentation on modern architecture.*

3 In conversation

Bonjour, je suis professeur Stein.
boñjoor, juh swee profesur stayeen

Hello, I'm Professor Stein.

De quelle université êtes-vous?
duh kel ooneevair-sitay et voo

What university are you from?

Je suis déléguée de l'université Paris II.
juh swee daylaygay duh looneevair-sitay paree duh

I'm the delegate from Paris II University.

4 Words to remember

Familiarize yourself with these words and then test yourself.

conference	**la conférence**	lah koñfayroñs
trade fair	**la foire-exposition**	lah fwar-ekspohseesyoñ
seminar	**le séminaire**	luh semeenair
lecture hall	**l'amphithéâtre** *(m)*	loñfeetayatruh
conference room	**la salle de conférences**	lah sal duh koñfayroñs
exhibition	**l'exposition** *(f)*	lekspohzeesyoñ
library	**la bibliothèque**	lah biblee-yotek
assistant professor	**le maître de conférences**	luh metruh duh koñfayroñs
professor	**le professeur**	luh profesur
medicine	**la médecine**	lah medseen
science	**la science**	lah siyoñs
literature	**la littérature**	lah leetairatyur
engineering	**l'ingénierie** *(f)*	lahjayneeuree

Nous avons un stand à la foire-exposition.
noo zavon uñ stond ah lah fwar ekspohseesyoñ
We have a stand at the trade fair.

5 Say it

I'm doing research in medicine.

I have a degree in literature.

She's the professor.

Quel est votre secteur?
kel ay votruh sektur

What's your field?

Je fais de la recherche en ingénierie.
juh fay duh lah reshairsh oñ lahjayneeuree

I'm doing research in engineering.

Comme c'est intéressant.
kom say añtayraysoñ

How interesting.

1 Warm up

Ask "Can I ...?"
(pp.34–5)

Say "I want to send an
email." (pp.80–1)

Ask "Can you send an
email?" (pp.80–1)

Les affaires
In business

You will receive a more friendly
reception and make a good impression
if you make the effort to begin a
meeting with a short introduction in
French, even if your vocabulary is
limited. After that, all parties will
probably be happy to continue the
meeting in English.

2 Words to remember

Familiarize yourself with these words and
then test yourself by concealing the French
with the cover flap.

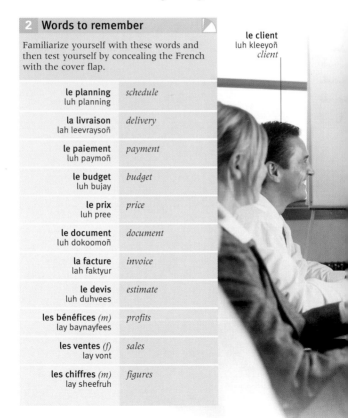

le client
luh kleeyoñ
client

le planning luh planning	*schedule*
la livraison lah leevraysoñ	*delivery*
le paiement luh paymoñ	*payment*
le budget luh bujay	*budget*
le prix luh pree	*price*
le document luh dokoomoñ	*document*
la facture lah faktyur	*invoice*
le devis luh duhvees	*estimate*
les bénéfices *(m)* lay baynayfees	*profits*
les ventes *(f)* lay vont	*sales*
les chiffres *(m)* lay sheefruh	*figures*

■■ **Cultural tip** In general, commercial
dealings are formal, but a lunch with wine is
still part of doing business in France. As a
client, you can expect to be taken out to a
restaurant, and as a supplier, you should
consider entertaining your customers.

3 Useful phrases

Memorize these phrases. Note that when asking *what...?* you use
quel(s) with masculine words but **quelle(s)** with feminine words.

On signe le contrat?
oñ seenuh luh koñtrah
*Shall we sign the
contract?*

le cadre
luh kadruh
executive

le contrat
luh koñtrah
contract

*Please send me the
contract.*

**Envoyez-moi le
contrat s'il vous plaît.**
oñvwayay mwah luh
koñtrah, seel voo play

*Have we agreed on a
schedule?*

**Nous sommes
convenus d'un
planning?**
noo som koñvunoo
duñ planning

*When can you make
the delivery?*

**Quand pouvez-vous
faire la livraison?**
koñ poovay voo fair lah
leevraysoñ

What's the budget?

Quel est le budget?
kel ay luh bujay

*Can you send me the
invoice?*

**Vous pouvez
m'envoyer la facture?**
voo poovay moñvwayay
lah faktyur

le rapport
luh rapor
report

4 Say it

Can you send me the estimate?

Have we agreed on a price?

What are the profits?

Réponses
Answers
Cover with flap

Révisez et répétez
Review and repeat

1 At the office

1 **l'agraffeuse**
lagrafurz

2 **la lampe**
lah lomp

3 **l'ordinateur portable**
lordeenatur portabluh

4 **le stylo**
luh steeloh

5 **le bureau**
luh byuroh

6 **le bloc-notes**
luh blok-not

7 **la pendule**
lah poñdool

1 At the office

Name these items.

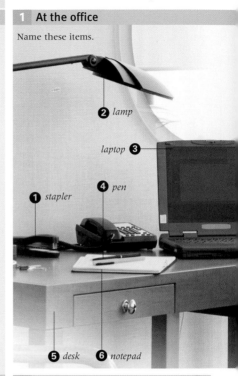

2 *lamp*

laptop 3

1 *stapler*   4 *pen*

5 *desk*   6 *notepad*

2 Jobs

1 **médecin**
medsañ

2 **plombier**
ploñbyay

3 **commerçant**
comairsoñ(oñt)

4 **comptable**
koñtabluh

5 **professeur**
profesur

6 **avocat**
avokah(aht)

2 Jobs

What are these jobs in French?

1 *doctor*

2 *plumber*

3 *shopkeeper*

4 *accountant*

5 *teacher*

6 *lawyer*

clock **7**

3 Work

Answer these questions following the English prompts.

Vous travaillez pour quelle compagnie?
1 Say "I work for myself."

De quelle université êtes-vous?
2 Say "I'm at the University of Bordeaux."

Quel est votre secteur?
3 Say "I'm doing medical research."

Nous sommes convenus d'un planning?
4 Say "Yes. Can you send me the budget?"

3 Work

1 **Je suis à mon compte.**
juh swee zah moñ koñt

2 **Je suis de l'université de Bordeaux.**
juh swee duh looneevair-sitay duh bordoe

3 **Je fais de la recherche en médecine.**
juh fay duh lah reshairsh oñ medseen

4 **Oui. Vous pouvez m'envoyer le budget?**
voo poovay moñvwayay lah bujay

4 How much?

Answer the question with the amount shown in brackets.

1 C'est combien le café? (€2.50)

2 C'est combien la chambre? (€47)

3 C'est combien pour un kilo de tomates? (€3.25)

4 C'est combien l'emplacement pour quatre jours? (€50)

4 How much?

1 **C'est deux euros cinquante.**
say duh zuroh sankont

2 **C'est quarante-sept euros.**
say sankont-set uroh

3 **C'est trois euros vingt-cinq**
say twrah zuroh vañ-sank

4 **C'est cinquante euros.**
say sankont uroh

1 Warm up

Say "I'm allergic to nuts." (pp.24–5)

Say the verb "avoir" (to have) in all its forms (je, tu, il/elle, vous, nous, ils/elles). (pp.14–15)

A la pharmacie
At the pharmacy

French pharmacists study for seven years before qualifying. They can give advice about minor health problems and are permitted to dispense a wide variety of medicines, even giving injections, if necessary. There is a duty pharmacist (**pharmacie de garde**) in most towns.

2 Match and repeat

Match the numbered items to the French words in the panel on the left and test yourself using the flap.

1 **le bandage**
   luh boñdarj

2 **le sirop**
   luh seeroe

3 **les gouttes** *(f)*
   lay goot

4 **le pansement**
   luh poñsumoñ

5 **la seringue**
   lah surañg

6 **la crème**
   lah krem

7 **le suppositoire**
   luh soopozitwar

8 **le cachet**
   luh kashay

bandage **1**   *syrup* **2**

drops **3**

4 *adhesive bandage*   *syringe* **5**

3 In conversation

Bonjour madame, vous désirez?
boñjoor, mad-dam. voo dayzeeray

Hello, madam. What would you like?

J'ai mal à l'estomac.
jay mal ah lestomah

I have a stomachache.

Vous avez la diarrhée?
voo zavay lah dyaray

Do you have diarrhea?

4 Words to remember

Familiarize yourself with these words and test yourself using the flap.

J'ai mal à la tête.
jay mal ah lah tet
I have a headache.

headache	**mal à la tête**	mal ah lah tet
stomachache	**mal à l'estomac**	mal ah lestomah
diarrhea	**la diarrhée**	lah dyaray
cold	**un rhume**	uñ room
cough	**une toux**	oon too
sunburn	**un coup de soleil**	uñ koo duh sol-lay
toothache	**mal aux dents**	mal oh doñ

6 Say it

I have a cold.

Do you have that as a cream?

Do you have a cough?

6 *cream*

7 *suppository*

8 *tablet*

5 Useful phrases

Familiarize yourself with these phrases and then test yourself using the cover flap.

I have a sunburn.	**J'ai un coup de soleil.** jay uñ koo duh sol-lay
Do you have that as tablets?	**Vous avez des cachets à la place?** voo zavay day kashay ah lah plas
I'm allergic to penicillin.	**Je suis allergique à la pénicilline.** juh swee zalurgeek ah lah peneesilin

Non, mais j'ai aussi mal à la tête.
noñ, may jay osee mal ah lah tet

No, but I also have a headache.

Prenez ça.
prunay sah

Take this.

Vous avez un sirop à la place?
voo zavay uh seeroe ah lah plas

Do you have that as a syrup?

Le corps
The body

1 Warm up

Say " I have a toothache" and "I have a sunburn." (pp.88–9)

Say the French for "red," "green," "black," and "yellow." (pp.74–5)

The most common phrase for talking about aches and pains is **J'ai mal à**… Don't forget that when **à** is placed in front of **le** it becomes **au** and in front of **les** it becomes **aux** (the "x" is silent). For example, **J'ai mal au dos** (*I have a backache*) and **J'ai mal aux oreilles** (*I have an earache*).

2 Match and repeat: body

Match the numbered parts of the body with the list on the left. Test yourself by using the cover flap.

1 **la main**
   lah mañ

2 **la tête**
   lah tet

3 **l'épaule** *(f)*
   laypoll

4 **le coude**
   luh kood

5 **les cheveux**
   lay shuhvuh

6 **le bras**
   luh brah

7 **le cou**
   luh koo

8 **la poitrine**
   lah pwatreen

9 **l'estomac** *(m)*
   lestomah

10 **la jambe**
   lah jomb

11 **le genou**
   luh juhnoo

12 **le pied**
   luh piyay

hand ❶
head ❷
shoulder ❸
❹ elbow
❺ hair
❻ arm
❼ neck
❽ chest
❾ stomach
❿ leg
⓫ knee
⓬ foot

3 Match and repeat: face

Match the numbered facial features with the list on the right.

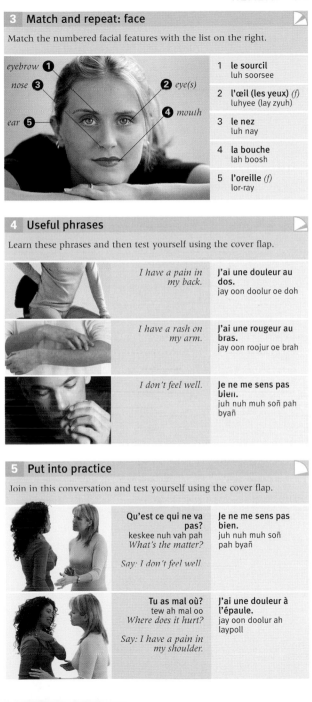

eyebrow **1**

nose **3**

2 *eye(s)*

4 *mouth*

ear **5**

1 **le sourcil**
   luh soorsee

2 **l'œil (les yeux)** *(f)*
   luhyee (lay zyuh)

3 **le nez**
   luh nay

4 **la bouche**
   lah boosh

5 **l'oreille** *(f)*
   lor-ray

4 Useful phrases

Learn these phrases and then test yourself using the cover flap.

	I have a pain in my back.	**J'ai une douleur au dos.** jay oon doolur oe doh
	I have a rash on my arm.	**J'ai une rougeur au bras.** jay oon roojur oe brah
	I don't feel well.	**Je ne me sens pas bien.** juh nuh muh soñ pah byañ

5 Put into practice

Join in this conversation and test yourself using the cover flap.

	Qu'est ce qui ne va pas? keskee nuh vah pah *What's the matter?* Say: *I don't feel well*	**Je ne me sens pas bien.** juh nuh muh soñ pah byañ
	Tu as mal où? tew ah mal oo *Where does it hurt?* Say: *I have a pain in my shoulder.*	**J'ai une douleur à l'épaule.** jay oon doolur ah laypoll

1 Warm up

Say "I need some tablets" and "He needs some cream." (pp.60–1 and pp.88–9)

What is the French for "I don't have a son"? (pp.10–15)

Chez le docteur
At the doctor

Unless it's an emergency, you have to make an appointment with the doctor and pay when you leave. You may be able to reclaim the money if you have medical insurance. You can find the names and addresses of local doctors from the local town hall or **syndicat d'initiative** (*tourist office*).

2 Useful phrases you may hear

Familiarize yourself with these phrases and then test yourself using the cover flap to conceal the French on the left.

Ce n'est pas sérieux. suh nay pah seryuh	*It's not serious.*
Vous avez besoin de tests. voo zavay buzwañ duh test	*You need to have tests.*
Vous avez une infection aux reins. voo zavay oon añfeksyoñ oh rañ	*You have a kidney infection.*
Vous avez besoin d'aller à l'hôpital. voo zavay buzwañ dalay ah lopeetal	*You need to go to the hospital.*

Vous prenez des médicaments?
voo prunay day maydikamoñ
Are you taking any medications?

3 In conversation

Qu'est-ce qui ne va pas?
keskee nuh vah pah

What's the matter?

J'ai une douleur à la poitrine.
jay oon doolur ah lah pwatreen

I have a pain in my chest.

Laissez-moi vous examiner.
lessay-mwah voo zekzaminay

Let me examine you.

🏳️ Cultural tip Before you go, find out if your health insurance covers emergency medical care in Europe; if it doesn't, buy a travel medical insurance policy. To call an ambulance in France, dial 15.

4 Useful phrases you may need to say

Practice these phrases and then test yourself using the cover flap.

Je suis enceinte.
juh swee zoñsant
I'm pregnant.

I'm diabetic.	**Je suis diabétique.** juh swee diyabeteek	
I'm epileptic.	**Je suis épileptique.** juh swee zepeelepteek	
I have asthma.	**Je suis asthmatique.** juh swee zasmateek	
I have a heart condition.	**J'ai un problème au cœur.** jay uñ prob-lem oh kur	
I feel faint.	**Je vais m'évanouir.** juh vay mayvanooweer	
I have a fever.	**J'ai de la fièvre.** jay duh lah fyevruh	
It's urgent.	**C'est urgent.** say turjoñ	

5 Say it

Do I need tests?

My son needs to go to the hospital.

It's not urgent.

C'est sérieux?
say seryuh

Is it serious?

Non, vous avez seulement une indigestion.
noñ, voo zavay surlmoñ oon añdeejestyoñ

No, you only have indigestion.

Quel soulagement!
kel soolarjemoñ

What a relief!

1 Warm up

Ask "How long is the trip?" (pp.42–3)

How do you ask "Do I need...?" (pp.92–3)

What is the French for "mouth" and "head"? (pp.90–1)

A l'hôpital
At the hospital

The main hospitals in France are attached to universities and are known as **Centres Hospitaliers Universitaires** (CHU). It is useful to know a few basic phrases relating to hospitals for use in an emergency or in case you need to visit a friend or colleague in the hospital.

2 Useful phrases

Familiarize yourself with these phrases. Conceal the French with the cover flap and test yourself.

Quelles sont les heures de visite? kel soñ lay zur duh vizeet	*What are the visiting hours?*	**l'intraveineuse** *(f)* lañtravaynurz *IV (intravenous drip)*
Ça va prendre combien de temps? sah vah prondruh koñbyañ duh toñ	*How long will it take?*	
Ça va faire mal? sah vah fair mal	*Will it hurt?*	
Allongez-vous ici, s'il vous plaît. aloñjay voo zeesee, seel voo play	*Please lie down here.*	
Vous ne devez pas manger. voo nuh duvay pah moñjay	*You must not eat.*	
Ne bougez pas la tête. nuh boojay pah lah tet	*Don't move your head.*	**Ça va mieux?** sah vah meeyuh *Are you feeling better?*
Ouvrez la bouche, s'il vous plaît. oovray lah boosh, seel voo play	*Please open your mouth.*	
Vous avez besoin d'une prise de sang. voo zavay buzwañ doon preez duh soñ	*You need a blood test.*	**Où est la salle d'attente?** oo ay lah sal datont *Where is the waiting room?*

3 Words to remember

Memorize these words and test yourself using the cover flap.

emergency room	**la salle des urgences** lah sal day zurjoñs
children's ward	**le service de pédiatrie** luh survees duh paydyah-tree
operating room	**la salle d'opération** lah sal dopairasyoñ
X-ray department	**la salle de radiologie** lah sal duh radyo-lojee
waiting room	**la salle d'attente** lah sal datont
elevator	**l'ascenseur** lasoñsur
stairs	**les escaliers** lay zeskalyay

Votre radio est normale.
votruh radyoh ay normal
Your X-ray is normal.

4 Put into practice

Join in this conversation. Read the French on the left and follow the instructions to make your reply. Then test yourself by concealing the answers with the cover flap.

Vous avez une infection.
voo zavay oon añfeksyoñ
You have an infection.

Ask: Do I need tests?

J'ai besoin de tests?
jay buzwañ duh test

Tout d'abord, vous avez besoin d'une prise de sang.
too dabor, voo zavay buzwañ doon preez duh soñ
First you will need a blood test.

Ask: Will it hurt?

Ça va faire mal?
sah vah fair mal

5 Say it

Does he need a blood test?

Where is the children's ward?

Do I need an X-ray?

Non, ne vous inquiétez pas.
noñ, nuh voo zañkyatay pah
No. Don't worry.

Ask: How long will it take?

Ça va prendre combien de temps?
sah vah prondruh koñbyañ duh toñ

Réponses
Answers
Cover with flap

Révisez et répétez
Review and repeat

1 The body

1 **la tête**
lah tet

2 **le bras**
luh brah

3 **la poitrine**
lah pwatreen

4 **l'estomac**
lestomah

5 **la jambe**
lah jomb

6 **le genou**
luh juhnoo

7 **le pied**
luh piyay

1 The body

Name the numbered body parts in French.

1 head
2 arm
chest **3**
4 stomach
leg **5**
6 knee
foot **7**

2 On the phone

1 **Je voudrais parler à Caroline Martin.**
juh voodray parlay ah karoleen martañ

2 **[your name] de l'imprimerie Laporte.**
[your name] duh lahpreemuree laport

3 **Je peux laisser un message?**
juh puh laysay uñ mesarj

4 **C'est bon pour le rendez-vous lundi à onze heures.**
say boñ poor luh roñday-voo lañdee ah onz ur

5 **Merci, au revoir.**
mairsee, ovwar

2 On the phone

You are arranging an appointment. Follow the conversation, replying in French following the English prompts.

Allô, société Apex.
1 *I'd like to speak to Caroline Martin.*

Oui, c'est de la part de qui?
2 *[your name] of Laporte printers.*

Je suis désolé, la ligne est occupée.
3 *Can I leave a message?*

Oui, bien sûr.
4 *The appointment on Monday at 11 am is fine.*

Très bien, au revoir.
5 *Thank you. Goodbye.*

3 Clothing

Say the French words for the numbered items of clothing.

jacket **2**

tie **1**

pants **3**

4 skirt

shoes **5**

pantyhose **6**

3 Clothing

1 **la cravate**
lah kravat

2 **la veste**
lah vest

3 **le pantalon**
luh poñtaloñ

4 **la jupe**
lah joop

5 **les chaussures**
lay shohsyur

6 **les collants**
lay kolloñ

4 At the doctor's

Say these phrases in French.

1 *I don't feel well.*

2 *Do I need tests?*

3 *I have a heart condition.*

4 *Do I need to go to the hospital?*

5 *I'm pregnant.*

4 At the doctor's

1 **Je ne me sens pas bien.**
juh nuh muh soñ pah byañ

2 **J'ai besoin de tests.**
jay buzwañ duh test

3 **J'ai un problème au cœur.**
jay uñ prob-lem oh kur

4 **J'ai besoin d'aller à l'hôpital.**
jay buzwañ dallay ah lopeetal

5 **Je suis enceinte.**
juh swee zoñsant

Say the months of the year in French. (pp.28–9)

Ask "Is there an art gallery?" (pp.48–9) and "How many brothers do you have?" (pp.14–15)

Chez nous
At home

Many city-dwellers live in an apartment block (**l'immeuble**), but in rural areas the houses tend to be single-family (**individuelle**). If you want to know the total number of rooms, you will need to ask "**Combien de pièces?**" If you want to know how many bedrooms, ask "**Combien de chambres?**"

2 Match and repeat

Match the numbered items to the list and test yourself using the flap.

1 **la fenêtre**
lah fenaytruh

2 **la cheminée**
lah shemnay

3 **le toit**
lah twut

4 **la gouttière**
lah gootyair

5 **le mur**
luh myur

6 **le volet**
luh volay

7 **la porte**
lah port

8 **le passage**
luh passarj

window **1**   chimney **2**

5 wall   **6** shutter   door **7**

🇫🇷 **Cultural tip** Most French houses have shutters ("volets") at each window. These are closed at night and in the heat of the day. Drapes, where they are present, tend to be more for decoration. A single-story bungalow is known as "un pavillon," and these are popular among the French as vacation homes in tourist resorts.

3 Words to remember

Familiarize yourself with these words and test yourself using the flap.

Quel est le loyer par mois?
kel ay luh lwayay par mwah?
What is the rent per month?

room	**la pièce** lah pies
floor	**le sol** luh sol
ceiling	**le plafond** luh plafoñ
bedroom	**la chambre** lah shombruh
bathroom	**la salle de bains** lah sal duh bañ
kitchen	**la cuisine** lah kwiseen
dining room	**la salle à manger** lah sal ah moñjay
living room	**le salon** luh saloñ
basement	**la cave** lah kav
attic	**le grenier** luh grunyay

 ❸ *roof*

❹ *gutter*

4 Useful phrases

Learn these phrases and test yourself.

Il y a un garage?
eelyah uh gararj

Is there a garage?

C'est disponible quand?
say deesponeebluh koñ

When is it available?

❽ *driveway*

C'est meublé?
say murblay

Is it furnished?

5 Say it

Is there a dining room?

Is it large?

Is it available in July?

Dans la maison
In the house

What is the French for "room" (pp.58–9), "desk" (pp.80–1), "bed" (pp.60–1), and "bathroom"? (pp.52–3)

How do you say "soft," "beautiful," and "big"? (pp.64–5)

When you rent a house or villa in France, it is usual to be asked to pay for services such as electricity and gas in addition to the basic weekly or monthly rent. Additional charges might also extend to wood or other fuel for an open fire, which is usually charged by the cubic meter.

2 Match and repeat

Match the numbered items to the list in the panel on the left. Then test yourself by concealing the French with the cover flap.

1 countertop

1 **le plan de travail**
luh plañ duh traveye

2 **l'évier** *(m)*
levyay

3 **le micro-ondes**
luh meekro-ond

4 **la cuisinière**
lah kwiseenyair

5 **le four**
luh foor

6 **le frigo**
luh freegoh

7 **la table**
lah tabluh

8 **la chaise**
lah shez

5 oven
6 refrigerator
4 stove
table **7**

3 In conversation

C'est le four.
say luh foor

This is the oven.

Il y a un lave-vaisselle aussi?
eelyah uñ lav-vaysel osee

Is there a dishwasher as well?

Oui, et il y a un grand congélateur.
wee, ay eelyah uñ groñ koñjelatur

Yes, and there's a big freezer.

4 Words to remember

Familiarize yourself with these words and test yourself using the flap.

Le canapé est neuf.
luh kanapay ay nurf
The sofa is new.

wardrobe	**l'armoire** *(f)* larmwar
armchair	**le fauteuil** luh fohtuhee
chest of drawers	**la commode** lah komohd
fireplace	**la cheminée** lah shemnay
carpet	**le tapis** luh tapee
bathtub	**la baignoire** lah bainwar
bathroom sink	**le lavabo** luh lavabo
drapes	**les rideaux** *(m)* lay ridoe

microwave ❸

❷ *sink*

❽ *chair*

6 Say it

Is there a microwave?

I like the fireplace.

What a soft sofa!

5 Useful phrases

Practice these phrases and then test yourself using the cover flap to conceal the French.

Is electricity included?	**L'électricité est inclue?** laylektreesitay et aňkloo
I don't like the drapes.	**Je n'aime pas les rideaux.** juh nem pah lay ridoe
The carpet is old.	**Le tapis est vieux.** luh tapee ay vyuh

L'évier est neuf?
levyay ay nurf

Is the sink new?

Bien sûr. Et voilà la machine à laver.
byaň syur. ay vwalah lah masheen ah lavay

Of course. And here's the washing machine.

Quel beau carrelage!
kel boe karlarj

What beautiful tiles!

1 Warm up

Say "I need," "you need," "he needs." (pp.64–5, pp.92–4)

What is the French for "day," "week," and "month"? (pp.28–9)

Say the days of the week. (pp.28–9)

Le jardin
The yard

The garden of a house or villa may be communal, or at least partly shared. Check with the rental agent or realtor. In general, French yards are well-kept and reasonably formal. The natural, "wild" look is not very popular and hedges are usually carefully trimmed and lawns regularly mown.

2 Words to remember

Familiarize yourself with these words and test yourself using the flap.

la tondeuse à gazon lah toñdurz ah gazoñ	*lawnmower*
la fourche lah foorsh	*fork*
la bêche lah besh	*spade*
le râteau luh ratoe	*rake*
la jardinerie lah jardañree	*garden center*

❷ *tree*

❸ *soil*

terrace **❶**

flowers **❼**   *weeds* **❽**   **❾** *path*

3 Useful phrases

Familarize yourself with these phrases and then test yourself.

The gardener comes once a week.	**Le jardinier vient une fois par semaine.** luh jardañyay vyañ oon fwah par suhmayn
Can you mow the lawn?	**Vous pouvez tondre la pelouse?** voo poovay toñdruh lah pelooz
Is the yard private?	**Le jardin est privé?** luh jardañ ay preevay
The garden needs watering.	**Le jardin a besoin d'eau.** luh jardañ ah buzwañ doe

4 Match and repeat

Match the numbered items to the words in the panel on the right.

4 *lawn* **5** *hedge* **6** *plants*

flower bed **10**

1 **la terrasse** lah terass

2 **l'arbre** *(m)* larbruh

3 **la terre** lah tair

4 **la pelouse** lah pelooz

5 **la haie** lah ay

6 **les plantes** *(f)* lay ploñt

7 **les fleurs** *(f)* lay flur

8 **les mauvaises herbes** *(f)* lay movay zurb

9 **l'allée** *(f)* lallay

10 **le parterre de fleurs** luh partair duh flur

5 Say it

The lawn needs watering.

Are there any trees?

The gardener comes on Fridays.

Les animaux
Pets

1 Warm up

Say "My name's John."
(pp.8–9)

How do you say "don't
worry"? (pp.94–5)

What's "your" in
French? (pp.12–13)

Half of all French households include
at least one pet, and most companion
animals are treated like members of
the family. There are slightly more
pet dogs than pet cats in France.
Fish and birds are also widely kept,
and rabbits and rodents are becoming
increasingly popular.

2 Match and repeat

Match the numbered animals to the French words
in the panel on the left. Then test yourself using
the cover flap.

1 **le chat**
luh shah

2 **le lapin**
luh lapañ

3 **l'oiseau** *(m)*
lwazoe

4 **le poisson**
luh pwassoñ

5 **le chien**
luh shiañ

6 **le hamster**
luh amstair

1 cat
2 rabbit
bird **3**
fish **4**
dog **5**
6 *hamster*

3 Useful phrases

Familiarize yourself with these phrases and then
test yourself using the cover flap.

Ce chien est gentil? suh shiañ ay joñtee	*Is this dog friendly?*
Je peux amener mon chien? juh puh amunay moñ shiañ	*Can I bring my dog?*
J'ai peur des chats. jay pur day shah	*I'm afraid of cats.*
Mon chien ne mord pas. moñ shiañ nuh mor pah	*My dog doesn't bite.*

Ce chat est plein de puces.
suh shah ay plañ
duh pous
This cat is full of fleas.

Cultural tip Many dogs in France are guard dogs, and you may encounter them tethered or roaming free. Approach farms and rural houses with care, and keep away from the dog's territory. Look out for warning notices such as "Attention au chien" (Beware of the dog).

ATTENTION AU CHIEN

---

4 Words to remember

Memorize these words and test yourself using the cover flap.

Mon chien est malade.
moñ shiañ ay malahd
My dog is not well.

vet	**le vétérinaire** luh vetairinair
vaccination	**la vaccination** lah vaksinasyoñ
pet passport	**le passeport d'animaux** luh passpor danimoe
basket	**le panier** luh panyay
cage	**la cage** lah karj
bowl	**la gamelle** lah gamel
collar	**le collier** luh kolyay
leash	**la laisse** lah less
fleas	**les puces** *(f)* lay pous

---

5 Put into practice

Join in this conversation. Read the French on the left and follow the instructions to make your reply. Then test yourself by concealing the answers with the cover flap.

C'est votre chien?
say votruh shiañ
Is this your dog?

Say: *Yes, his name is Sandy.*

Oui, il s'appelle Sandy.
wee, eel sapell Sandy

J'ai peur des chiens.
jay pur day shiañ
I'm afraid of dogs.

Say: *Don't worry. He's friendly.*

Ne vous inquiétez pas. Il est gentil.
nuh voo zañkyatay pah. eel ay joñtee

Révisez et répétez
Review and repeat

1 Colors

1 **noir**
nwar

2 **blanche**
blonsh

3 **rouge**
rooj

4 **verte**
vairt

5 **jaunes**
jon

1 Colors

Complete the sentences with the French for the color in brackets. Be careful to choose the correct masculine or feminine form.

1 **Vous avez cette veste en _____ ?** *(black)*

2 **Je prends la jupe _____ .** *(white)*

3 **Vous avez cette robe en _____ ?** *(red)*

4 **Non mais j'ai une _____ .** *(green)*

5 **Vous avez des chaussettes _____ ?** *(yellow)*

2 Kitchen

1 **la cuisinière**
lah kwiseenyair

2 **le frigo**
luh freegoh

3 **l'évier**
levyay

4 **le micro-ondes**
luh meekro-ond

5 **le four**
luh foor

6 **la chaise**
lah shez

7 **la table**
lah tabluh

2 Kitchen

Say the French words for the numbered items.

❶ stove

refrigerator ❷

oven ❺

chair ❻

3 House

You are visiting a house in France. Join in
the conversation, replying in French
following the English prompts.

Voilà le salon.
1 *What a pretty fireplace!*

Oui, et il y a aussi une grande cuisine.
2 *How many bedrooms?*

Il y a trois chambres.
3 *Do you have a garage?*

Non, mais il y a un grand jardin.
4 *When is it available?*

Juillet.
5 *What is the rent per month?*

3 House

1 **Quelle belle
  cheminée!**
  kel bel shemnay

2 **Combien de
  chambres?**
  koñbyañ duh
  shombruh

3 **Vous avez un
  garage?**
  voo zavay uñ
  gararj

4 **C'est disponible
  quand?**
  say
  deesponeebluh
  koñ

5 **Quel est le loyer
  par mois?**
  kel ay luh lwayay
  par mwah

4 At home

Say the French for
the following
items:

1 *washing machine*

2 *sofa*

3 *attic*

4 *dining room*

5 *tree*

6 *garden*

4 At home

1 **la machine à
  laver**
  lah masheen ah
  lavay

2 **le canapé**
  luh kanapay

3 **le grenier**
  luh grunyay

4 **la salle à manger**
  lah sal ah moñjay

5 **l'arbre**
  larbruh

6 **le jardin**
  luh jardañ**

1 Warm up

Ask "How do I get to the bank?" and "How do I get to the post office?" (pp.68–9)

What's the French for "passport"? (pp.54–5)

Ask "What time?" (pp.30–1)

La poste et la banque
Mail and banks

The post office also serves as a bank. You do not usually need to wait in line for a teller, since there are normally ATMs available outside the building. Stamps are also available from **le tabac** (*bar/tobacconists*).

2 Words to remember: mail

Familiarize yourself with these words and test yourself using the cover flap to conceal the French on the left.

la boîte postale lah bwat post-tal	*mailbox*
la carte postale lah kart post-tal	*postcard*
le colis luh kolee	*package*
par avion par avyoñ	*air mail*
en recommandé oñ rukomoñday	*registered mail*
le timbre luh tambruh	*stamp*
le code postal luh kod post-tal	*postal (ZIP) code*
le facteur luh faktur	*mail carrier*

C'est combien pour le Royaume-Uni?
say koñbyañ poor luh royom oonee
How much is it for the United Kingdom?

l'enveloppe *(f)*
loñvuhlop
envelope

3 In conversation

Je voudrais retirer de l'argent.
juh voodray ruteeray duh larjoñ

I'd like to withdraw some money.

Vous avez une identification?
voo zavay oon eedoñtee-fikasyoñ

Do you have any identification?

Oui, voilà mon passeport.
wee, vwalah moñ passpor

Yes, here's my passport.

4 Words to remember: banks

Familiarize yourself with these words and test yourself using the cover flap to conceal the French on the right.

la carte bancaire
lah kart boñkair
debit card

Comment je peux payer?
komon juh puh payay
How can I pay?

PIN	**le code** luh kod	
bank	**la banque** lah boñk	
teller	**le guichet** luh geeshay	
notes	**les billets** lay beeyay	
ATM	**le distributeur automatique** luh distreebootur otomateek	
traveler's checks	**les chèques de voyage** lay shek duh vwoyarj	

5 Useful phrases

Learn these phrases and then test yourself using the cover flap.

6 Say it

I'd like a stamp for a postcard.

I'd like to cash some traveler's checks.

Do I need my passport?

I'd like to change some money.	**Je voudrais changer de l'argent.** juh voodray shoñjay duh larjoñ
What is the exchange rate?	**Quel est le taux de change?** kel ay luh toe duh shonj
I'd like to withdraw some money.	**Je voudrais retirer de l'argent.** juh voodray ruteeray duh larjoñ

Composez votre code s'il vous plaît.
komposay votruh kod seel voo play

Please type in your PIN.

J'ai besoin de signer aussi?
jay buzwañ duh seenyay ohsee

Do I need to sign, too?

Non, ce n'est pas nécessaire.
noñ, suh nay pah nesesair

No, that's not necessary.

Les services
Services

What's the French for "doesn't work"? (pp.60–1)

Say "today" and "tomorrow." (pp.28–9)

You can combine the French words on these pages with the vocabulary you learned in week 10 to help you explain basic problems and cope with arranging most repairs. When negotiating building work or a repair, it's a good idea to agree on the price and method of payment in advance.

2 Words to remember

Familiarize yourself with these words and test yourself using the flap.

le plombier luh ploñbyay	*plumber*
l'électricien (m) laylektreesyañ	*electrician*
le garagiste luh gararjeest	*mechanic*
le constructeur luh koñstruktur	*builder, handyman*
la femme de ménage lah fam duh maynarj	*cleaner*
le décorateur luh daykoratur	*decorator*
le charpentier luh sharpañtyay	*carpenter*
le maçon luh massoñ	*bricklayer*

la manivelle lah maneevel *tire iron*

Je n'ai pas besoin d'un garagiste. juh nay pah buzwañ duñ gararjeest *I don't need a mechanic.*

3 In conversation

La machine à laver est en panne. lah masheen ah lavay ay toñ pan

The washing machine has broken down.

Oui, le tuyeau est cassé. wee luh tweeyoh ay kassay

Yes, the hose is broken.

Vous pouvez la réparer? voo poovay lah rayparay

Can you repair it?

4 Useful phrases

Learn these phrases and then test yourself using the cover flap.

Please clean the bathroom.

Nettoyez la salle de bain, s'il vous plait.
netwuhyay lah sal duh bañ seel voo play

Can you repair the boiler?

Vous pouvez réparer la chaudière?
voo poovay rayparay lah shodyair

Do you know a good electrician?

Vous connaissez un bon électricien?
voo konessay uñ boñ aylektreesyañ

Je peux faire réparer ça où?
juh puh fair rayparay sah oo
Where can I get this repaired?

5 Put into practice

Practice these phrases. Cover up the text on the right and complete the dialogue in French. Check your answers and repeat if necessary.

Votre clôture est cassée.
votruh klotoor ay kassay
Your fence is broken.

Ask: *Do you know a good handyman?*

Vous connaissez un bon constructeur?
voo konessay uh boñ koñstruktur

Oui, il y en a un dans le village.
wee, eelyonah uñ doñ luh villarj
Yes, there is one in the village.

Ask: *Do you have his phone number?*

Vous avez son numéro de téléphone?
voo zavay soñ noomairoe duh telayfon

Non, vous avez besoin d'un nouveau.
noñ. voo zavay buzwañ duñ noovoh

No, you need a new one.

Vous pouvez faire ça aujourd'hui?
voo poovay fair sah ohjoordwee

Can you do it today?

Non, je reviens demain.
non, juh ruvyañ dumañ

No. I'll come back tomorrow.

1 Warm up

Say the days of the week in French. (pp.28–9)

How do you say "cleaner"? (pp.110–11)

Say "It's 9:30," "10:45," and "12:00." (pp.10–11, pp.30–1)

Venir
To come

The verb **venir** (*to come*) is another important verb. Other useful verbs are made up of **venir** with a prefix, such **revenir** (*to come back*) and **devenir** (*to become*). These can be formed in the same way as **venir** (below). Remember that **je viens** can mean either *I come* or *I am coming*.

2 Venir: to come

Say the different forms of **venir** (*to come*) aloud. Use the cover flap to test yourself and, when you are confident, practice the sample sentences below.

je viens juh vyañ	*I come*
tu viens tew vyañ	*you come (informal singular)*
il/elle vient eel/el vyañ	*he/she comes*
nous venons noo vunoñ	*we come*
vous venez voo vunay	*you come (formal singular or plural)*
ils/elles viennent eel/el vyen	*they come*
Je viens de New York. juh vyañ duh noo york	*I come from New York.*
Nous venons tous les mardis. noo vunoñ too lay mardee	*We come every Tuesday.*
Ils viennent par le train. eel vyen par luh trañ	*They come by train.*

Il vient de Chine.
eel vyañ duh sheen
He comes from China.

🔵⚪🔴 **Conversational tip** You can use the phrase "je viens de..." (literally "I come from...") to talk about something you have just done or have recently completed—for example, "je viens de faire les courses" (I have just gone shopping) or "je viens d'envoyer un email" (I have just sent an email).
To say "just" in the sense of "only," as in "I eat just a sandwich for lunch," the French use "seulement": "Je mange seulement un sandwich pour déjeuner."

3 Useful phrases

Learn these phrases and then test yourself using the cover flap.

Je viens de me réveiller.
juh vyañ duh
muh rayvay-yay
I have just woken up.

When can I come?	**Je peux venir quand?** juh puh vuneer koñ
Where does she come from?	**Elle vient d'où?** el vyañ doo
The cleaner comes every Monday.	**La femme de ménage vient tous les lundis.** lah fam duh maynarj vyañ too lay luñdee
Come with me. (informal/formal)	**Viens avec moi./ Venez avec moi.** vyañ avek mwah/ vunay avek mwah

4 Put into practice

Join in this conversation. Read the French on the left and follow the instructions to make your reply. Then test yourself by concealing the answers with the cover flap.

Bonjour, salon de coiffure Christine.
boñjoor, saloñ duh kwafur Christine
Hello, this is Christine's hair salon.

Say: *I'd like an appointment.*

Je voudrais un rendez-vous.
juh voodray uñ roñday-voo

Vous voulez venir quand?
voo voolay vuneer koñ
When do you want to come?

Say: *Can I come today?*

Je peux venir aujourd'hui?
juh puh vuneer oh-joordwee

Oui bien sûr, à quelle heure?
wee byañ syur, ah kel ur
Yes, of course. What time?

Say: *At 10:30.*

A dix heures et demie.
ah deez ur ay dumee

La police et le crime
Police and crime

1 Warm up

What's the French for "big/tall" and "small/short"? (pp.64–5)

Say "The room is big" and "The bed is small." (pp.64–5)

While in France, if you are the victim of a crime, you report it to the police. In an emergency, reach them by dialing 17. You may have to explain your problem in French, at least initially, so some basic vocabulary is useful. In the event of a burglary, the police will usually come to the house.

2 Words to remember: crime

Familiarize yourself with these words.

le cambriolage luh kañbryolarj	*burglary*
le rapport de police luh rapor duh polees	*police report*
le voleur luh volur	*thief*
la police lah polees	*police*
la déposition lah daypoziyoñ	*statement*
le témoin luh taymwañ	*witness*
l'avocat(e) lavokah(aht)	*lawyer*

J'ai besoin d'un avocat.
jay buzwañ duñ avokah
I need a lawyer.

3 Useful phrases

Memorize these phrases and then test yourself using the cover flap.

J'ai été cambriolé(e). jay aytay kañbryolay	*I've been burgled.*
Qu'est-ce qui a été volé? keskee ah aytay volay	*What was stolen?*
Vous avez vu qui a fait ça? voo zavay voo kee ah fay sah	*Did you see who did it?*
Ça s'est passé quand? sah say passay koñ	*When did it happen?*

l'appareil-photo
lapareye foto
camera

le porte-monnaie
luh port mohnay
wallet

4 Words to remember: appearance

Learn these words. Remember, some adjectives have a feminine form.

Il est chauve avec une barbe.
eel ay shohv avek oon barb
He is bald and has a beard.

Il a les cheveux noirs et courts.
eel ah lay shuvuh nwar ay kor
He has short, black hair.

man	**l'homme** *(m)* lom
woman	**la femme** lah fam
tall	**grand/grande** groñ/groñd
short	**petit/petite** puhtee/puhteet
young	**jeune** juhn
old	**vieux/vieille** vyuh/vyay
fat	**gros/grosse** groe/gros
thin	**maigre** maygruh
long/short hair	**les cheveux longs/ courts** *(m)* lay shuvuh loñ/kor
glasses	**les lunettes** *(f)* lay loonet
beard	**la barbe** lah barb

Cultural tip In France there is a difference between "la gendarmerie" and "la police." La gendarmerie operates in smaller towns and la police in major cities. Their appearance and uniform are similar and officers from both forces carry guns.

---

5 Put into practice

Practice these phrases. Then cover up the text on the right and follow the instructions to make your reply in French.

Il ressemblait à quoi?
eel ruzoñblay ah kwah
What did he look like?

Say: Short and fat.

Petit et gros.
puhtee ay groe

Et les cheveux?
ay lay shuvuh
And his hair?

Say: Long, with a beard.

Longs avec une barbe.
loñ avek oon barb

Révisez et répétez
Review and repeat

Réponses
Answers
Cover with flap

1 To come

1 **viens**
vyañ

2 **vient**
vyañ

3 **venons**
vunoñ

4 **venez**
vunay

5 **viennent**
vyen

1 To come

Fill in the blanks with the correct form of **venir** (*to come*).

1 Je _____ à quatre heures.

2 Le jardinier _____ une fois par semaine.

3 Nous _____ pour déjeuner mardi.

4 Vous _____ avec nous?

5 Mes parents _____ par le train.

2 Bank and mail

1 **les billets**
lay biyay

2 **les timbres**
lay tambruh

3 **la carte bancaire**
lah kart boñkair

4 **les cartes postales**
lay kart post-tal

5 **le colis**
luh kolee

2 Bank and mail

Say the French words for the following numbered items:

1 *bills*

2 *stamps*

3 *debit card*

4 *postcards*

package **5**

3 Appearance

What do these descriptions mean?

1 **C'est un homme grand et maigre.**

2 **Elle a les cheveux courts et des lunettes.**

3 **Je suis petite et j'ai les cheveux longs.**

4 **Elle est vieille et grosse.**

5 **Il a les yeux bleus et une barbe.**

3 Appearance

1 *He's a tall, thin man.*

2 *She has short hair and glasses.*

3 *I'm short and I have long hair.*

4 *She is old and fat.*

5 *He has blue eyes and a beard.*

4 The pharmacy

You are asking a pharmacist for advice. Join in the conversation, replying in French following the English prompts.

Bonjour. Je peux vous aider?
1 *I have a cough.*

Et vous avez aussi un rhume?
2 *No, but I have a headache.*

Prenez ces cachets.
3 *Do you have that as a syrup?*

Bien sûr. Voilà.
4 *Thank you. How much is that?*

Six euros.
5 *Here you are. Goodbye.*

4 The pharmacy

1 **J'ai une toux.**
jay oon too

2 **Non, mai j'ai mal à la tête.**
noñ, may jay mal ah lah tet

3 **Vous avez un sirop à la place?**
voo zavay uñ seeroe ah lah plas

4 **Merci. C'est combien?**
mairsee. say koñbyañ

5 **Voilà. Au revoir.**
vwalah. ovwar

Les loisirs
Leisure time

The French pride themselves on their support for the arts, including opera and film. It would not be unusual to number politics or philosophy among your interests. Phrasebooks aimed at French speakers often have a section on useful conversational openers for these topics.

2 Words to remember

Familiarize yourself with these words and test yourself using the cover flap to conceal the French on the left.

le théâtre luh tay-atruh	*theater*
le cinéma luh sinaymah	*movie theater*
la discothèque lah diskotek	*disco*
la musique lah moozeek	*music*
l'art *(m)* lar	*art*
le sport luh spor	*sports*
le tourisme luh torizmuh	*sightseeing*
les jeux vidéos lay juh viday-oh	*computer games*

J'adore l'opéra.
jador lopayra
I love opera.

les spectateurs *(m)*
lay spektahtur
audience

3 In conversation

Salut, tu veux jouer au tennis aujourd'hui?
saloo, tew vuh jooay oh tenees oh-joordwee

Hi, do you want to play tennis today?

Non. Je n'aime pas le sport.
noñ. juh nem pah luh spor

No, I don't like sports.

Alors, quels sont tes intérêts?
alor, kel soñ tay zañtairay

So what are your interests?

4 Useful phrases

Learn these phrases and then test yourself using the cover flap.

	What are your (formal/informal) interests?	**Quels sont vos/tes intérêts?** kel soñ voe/tay zañtayray
	I like the theater.	**J'aime le théâtre.** jem luh tay-atruh
	I prefer the movies.	**Je préfère le cinéma.** juh prayfair luh sinaymah
	I'm interested in art.	**Je m'intéresse à l'art.** juh mañtairess ah lar
	That bores me.	**Ça m'ennuie.** sah moñwee

Je déteste la guitare.
juh daytest lah geetar
I hate guitar music.

la galerie
lah galuree
balcony

l'orchestre *(m)*
lorkestruh
orchestra

5 Say it

I'm interested in music.

I prefer sports.

I don't like computer games.

Je préfère le shopping.
juh prayfair luh shopping

I prefer shopping.

Ça ne m'intéresse pas.
sah nuh mañtairess pah

That doesn't interest me.

Pas de problème. J'y vais toute seule.
pah de prob-lem. jee vay toot surl

No problem. I'll go on my own.

1 Warm up

Ask "Do you (formal) want to play tennis?" (pp.118–19)

Say "I like the theater" and "I prefer sightseeing." (pp.118–19)

Say "That doesn't interest me." (pp.118–19)

Le sport et les passe-temps
Sports and hobbies

The verb **faire** (*to do or to make*) is a useful verb for talking about hobbies. **Faire** is followed by **du**, **de la** or **de l'**: **Je fais de la peinture** (*I paint*). You can also use the verb **jouer** (*to play*) when talking about playing sports and music.

2 Words to remember

Memorize these words and then test yourself.

le football/rugby luh futbohl/roogbee	*soccer/rugby*
le tennis luh tenees	*tennis*
la natation lah natasyoñ	*swimming*
la voile lah vwal	*sailing*
la pêche lah pesh	*fishing*
la peinture lah pañtyur	*painting*
le vélo luh vaylo	*cycling*
la randonnée lah rañdonay	*hiking*

le bunker
luh bañkuh
bunker

le joueur de golf
luh joowur duh golf
golfer

Je joue au golf tout les jours.
juh joo oh golf too lay joor
I play golf every day.

3 Useful phrases

Familiarize yourself with these phrases.

Je fais du rugby. juh fay doo roogbee	*I play rugby.*
Il joue au tennis. eel joo oh tenees	*He plays tennis.*
Elle fait de la peinture. el fay duh lah pañtyur	*She paints.*

4 Faire: to do or to make

The verb **faire** (*to do or to make*) is also used to describe the weather. Learn its different forms and practice the sample sentences below.

Il fait beau aujourd'hui.
eel fay boe oh-joordwee
It's nice out today.

I do	**je fais** juh fay
you do (informal)	**tu fais** tew fay
he/she does	**il/elle fait** eel/el fay
we do	**nous faisons** noo fayzon
you do (formal/plural)	**vous faites** voo fet
they do	**ils/elles font** eel/el foñ
I go hiking.	**Je fais de la randonnée.** juh fay duh lah rañdonay
What do you do?	**Que faites-vous?** kuh fet voo
We play tennis.	**Nous faisons du tennis.** noo fayzon doo tenees

le drapeau
luh drapoh
flag

le parcours de golf
luh parkoor duh golf
golf course

5 Put into practice

Practice these phrases. Then cover up the text on the right and complete the dialogue in French. Check your answers.

Qu'est-ce que vous aimez faire?
keskuh voo zemay fair
What do you like doing?

Say: I like playing tennis.

J'aime jouer au tennis.
jem jooway oh tenees

Tu fais du football aussi?
tew fay doo futbohl ohsee
Do you play soccer, too?

Say: No. I play rugby.

Non, je fais du rugby.
noñ, juh fay doo roogbee

Cultural tip France boasts a huge variety of regional games, such as pelota in the Basque country. Most popular of all, the French version of bowls—"pétanque" or "boules"—is played in almost every town and village.

1 Warm up

Say "my husband" and "my wife." (pp.10–11)

How do you say "lunch" and "dinner" in French? (pp.20–1)

Say "Sorry, I'm busy." (pp.32–3)

Voir des gens
Socializing

The French dinner table is the center of the social world. You can expect to do a lot of your socializing enjoying food and wine. It is best to use the more polite **vous** form to talk to people you meet socially until they call you **tu**, in which case you can reciprocate.

2 Useful phrases

Learn these phrases and then test yourself.

Je voudrais vous inviter à dîner. juh voodray voo zañveetay ah deenay	*I'd like to invite you for dinner.*
Vous êtes libre mercredi prochain? voo zet leebruh mairkrudee prochen	*Are you free next Wednesday?*
Une autre fois peut-être. oon awtruh fwah putetruh	*Another time, perhaps.*

Cultural tip When you go to someone's house for the first time, it is usual to bring flowers or wine. If you are invited again, having seen your host's house, you can bring something a little more personal.

3 In conversation

Vous voulez venir dîner mardi?
voo voolay vuneer deenay mardee

Would you like to come to dinner on Tuesday?

Je suis désolée, je suis occupée.
juh swee dayzolay, juh swee zokoopay

I'm sorry, I'm busy.

Pourquoi pas jeudi?
poorkwah pah jurdee

What about Thursday?

4 Words to remember

Familiarize yourself with these words and test yourself using the flap.

l'hôtesse (f)
lohtess
hostess

l'invitée (f)
lanveetay
guest

party	**la soirée** lah swaray
dinner party	**le dîner** luh deenay
invitation	**l'invitation** lañveetasyoñ
reception	**la réception** lah raysepsyoñ
cocktail party	**le cocktail** luh koktail

5 Put into practice

Join in this conversation.

Vous pouvez venir à une réception ce soir.
voo poovay vuneer ah oon raysepsyoñ suh swah
Can you come to a reception this evening?

Say: Yes, I'd love to.

Oui, avec plaisir.
wee, avek playzeer

Ça commence à huit heures.
sah komoñs ah weet ur
It starts at eight o'clock.

Ask: Should I dress formally?

Il faut s'habiller?
eel foe sabeeyay

Merci de nous avoir invités.
mairsee duh noo zavwar añveetay
Thank you for inviting us.

Avec plaisir.
avek playzeer

I'd love to.

Venez avec votre mari.
vunay avek votruh maree

Please bring your husband.

Merci. A quelle heure?
mairsee. ah kel ur

Thank you. What time?

Révisez et répétez
Review and repeat

1 Animals

1 **le poisson**
luh pwassoñ

2 **l'oiseau**
lwazoe

3 **le lapin**
luh lapañ

4 **le chat**
luh shah

5 **le hamster**
luh amstair

6 **le chien**
luh shiañ

1 Animals

Say the French words for the numbered animals.

fish ❶

bird ❷

cat ❹

hamster ❺

2 I like...

1 **J'aime le rugby.**
jem luh roogbee

2 **Je n'aime pas
le golf.**
juh nem pah
luh golf

3 **J'aime faire de
la peinture.**
jem fair duh
lah pañtyur

4 **Je n'aime pas
jouer aux boules.**
juh nem pah
jooway oh bool

2 I like...

Say the following in French:

1 *I like rugby.*

2 *I don't like golf.*

3 *I like painting.*

4 *I don't like playing
boules.*

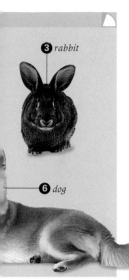

3 *rabbit*

6 *dog*

3 To do

Use the correct form of the verb **faire** in these sentences.

1 Tu _____ de la pêche?

2 Elle _____ de la voile.

3 Que _____ vous?

4 Il _____ froid aujourd'hui.

5 Vous _____ de la randonnée?

6 J'aime _____ de la natation.

3 To do

1 **fais**
fay

2 **fait**
fay

3 **faites**
fet

4 **fait**
fay

5 **faites**
fet

6 **faire**
fair

4 An invitation

You are invited for dinner. Join in the conversation, replying in French following the English prompts.

Vous voulez venir pour déjeuner vendredi?
1 *I'm sorry, I'm busy.*

Pourquoi pas samedi?
2 *I'd love to.*

Venez avec vos enfants.
3 *Thank you. At what time?*

A douze heures et demie.
4 *That's good for me.*

4 An invitation

1 **Je suis désolé(e), je suis occupé(e).**
juh swee dayzolay, juh swee zokoopay

2 **Avec plaisir.**
avek playzeer

3 **Merci. A quelle heure?**
mairsee, ah kel ur

4 **C'est bon pour moi.**
say boñ poor mwah

Reinforce and progress

Regular practice is the key to maintaining and advancing your language skills. In this section you will find a variety of suggestions for reinforcing and extending your knowledge of French. Many involve returning to exercises in the book and using the dictionaries to extend their scope. Go back through the lessons in a different order, mix and match activities to make up your own 15-minute daily program, or focus on topics that are of particular relevance to your current needs.

Keep warmed up
Revisit the Warm Up boxes to remind yourself of key words and phrases. Make sure you work your way through all of them on a regular basis.

1 Warm up

Say "I'm sorry" (pp.32–3).

What is the French for "I'd like an appointment" (pp.32–3)?

How do you say "who?" in French (pp.32–3)?

2 I'd like...

Say you'd like the following:

jam **2**   bread **3**

1 black coffee

large coffee with milk **4**

Review and repeat again
Work through a Review and Repeat lesson as a way of reinforcing words and phrases presented in the course. Return to the main lesson for any topic on which you are no longer confident.

3 In conversation: taxi

Carry on conversing
Reread the In Conversation panels. Say both parts of the conversation, paying attention to the pronunciation. Where possible, try incorporating new words from the dictionary.

Le marché aux fromages, s'il vous plaît.
luh marshayoe fromarj, seel voo play

The cheese market, please.

Oui, sans problème, monsieur.
wee, soñ problem musyuh

Yes, no problem, sir.

Vous pouvez me déposer ici, s'il vous plaît?
voo poovay muh daypoasay eesee, seel voo play

Can you drop me here, please?

4 Useful phrases

Learn these phrases and then test yourself using the flap.

Ouvert	What time do you open/close?	Vous ouvrez/fermez à quelle heure? voo oovray/fairmay ah kel ur
Toilettes	Where are the restrooms?	Où sont les toilettes? oo soh lay twalet
	Is there wheelchair access?	Il y a un accès pour les chaises roulantes? eelyah uñ aksay poor lay shez roolant

Practice phrases
Return to the Useful Phrases and Put into Practice exercises. Test yourself using the cover flap. When you are confident, devise your own versions of the phrases, using new words from the dictionary.

Match, repeat, and extend
Remind yourself of words related to specific topics by returning to the Match and Repeat and Words to Remember exercises. Test yourself using the cover flap. Discover new words in that area by referring to the dictionary and menu guide.

5 Match and repeat

Match the numbered items in this scene with the text in the panel.

❷ *lettuce*

❸ *lemons*

❹ *leeks*

❶ *zucchini*

1 **les courgettes** *(f)*
lay korjet

2 **la salade**
lah sal-lad

3 **les citrons** *(m)*
lay sitroñ

4 **les poireaux** *(m)*
lay pwaroe

5 **les tomates** *(f)*
lay toemat

6 **les champignons** *(m)*
lay shoñpiyoñ

7 **les avocats** *(m)*
läy žavocah

8 **les pommes de terre** *(f)*
lay pom duh tair

tomatoes ❺

mushrooms ❻

❼ *avocados*

❽ *potatoes*

6 Say it

The lawn needs watering.

Are there any trees?

The gardener comes on Fridays.

Say it again
The Say It exercises are a useful instant reminder for each lesson. Practice these, using your own vocabulary variations from the dictionary or elsewhere in the lesson.

Using other resources

In addition to working with this book, try the following language extension ideas:

- Visit a French-speaking country and try out your new skills with native speakers. Find out if there is a French community near you. There may be stores, cafés, restaurants, and clubs. Try to visit some of these and use your French to order food and drink and strike up conversations. Most native speakers will be happy to speak French to you.

- Join a language class or club. There are usually evening and day classes available at a variety of different levels. Or you could start a club yourself if you have friends who are also interested in keeping up their French.

- Look at French magazines and newspapers. The pictures will help you to understand the text. Advertisements are also a useful way of expanding your vocabulary.

- Use the Internet, where you can find all kinds of websites for learning languages, some of which offer free online help and activities. You can also find French websites for everything from renting a house to shampooing your pet. You can even access French radio and TV stations online. Start by going to a French search engine, such as *voila.fr*, and key in a subject that interests you, or set yourself a challenge: for example, finding a two-bedroom house for rent by the sea in Normandy.

Menu guide

This guide lists the most common terms you may encounter on French menus or when shopping for food. If you can't find an exact phrase, try looking up its component parts.

A

abats *offal*
abricot *apricot*
à emporter *to go*
agneau *lamb*
aiguillette de bœuf *slices of rump steak*
ail *garlic*
ailloli *garlic mayonnaise*
à la broche *spit roast*
à la jardinière *with assorted vegetables*
à la normande *in cream sauce*
à la vapeur *steamed*
amande *almond*
ananas *pineapple*
anchois *anchovies*
andouillette *spicy sausage*
anguille *eel*
à point *medium*
artichaut *artichoke*
asperge *asparagus*
assiette anglaise *selection of cold meats*
au gratin *baked in a milk, cream, and cheese sauce*
au vin blanc *in white wine*
avocat *avocado*

B

banane *banana*
barbue *brill (fish)*
bavaroise *light mousse*
béarnaise *with béarnaise sauce*
bécasse *woodcock*
béchamel *white sauce*
beignet *fritter, doughnut*
beignet aux pommes *apple fritter*
betterave *beet*
beurre *butter*
beurre d'anchois *anchovy paste*
beurre noir *dark, melted butter*
bien cuit *well done*
bière *beer*
bière à la pression *draft beer*
bière blonde *lager*
bière brune *bitter beer*
bière panachée *beer with soda*
bifteck *steak*
bisque d'écrevisses *crayfish soup*

bisque de homard *lobster soup*
biscuit de Savoie *sponge cake*
blanquette de veau *veal stew*
bleu *very rare*
bleu d'auvergne *blue cheese from Auvergne*
bœuf bourguignon *beef cooked in red wine*
bœuf braisé *braised beef*
bœuf en daube *beef casserole*
bœuf miroton *beef and onion stew*
bœuf mode *beef stew with carrots*
bolet *boletus (mushroom)*
boudin blanc *white pudding*
boudin noir *black pudding*
bouillabaisse *fish soup*
bouilli *boiled*
bouillon *broth*
bouillon de légumes *vegetable stock*
bouillon de poule *chicken stock*
boulette *meatball*
bouquet rose *shrimp*
bourride *fish soup*
brandade *cod in cream and garlic*
brioche *round roll*
brochet *pike*
brochette *kebab*
brugnon *nectarine*
brûlot *flambéed brandy*
brut *very dry*

C

cabillaud *cod*
café *coffee (black)*
café au lait *coffee with milk*
café complet *continental breakfast*
café crème *coffee with milk*
café glacé *iced coffee*
café liégeois *iced coffee with cream*
caille *quail*
calamar/calmar *squid*
calvados *apple brandy*
canapé *small open sandwich, canapé*

canard *duck*
canard laqué *Peking duck*
caneton *duckling*
cantal *white cheese from Auvergne*
câpres *capers*
carbonnade *beef cooked in beer*
cari *curry*
carotte *carrot*
carottes Vichy *carrots in butter and parsley*
carpe *carp*
carré d'agneau *rack of lamb*
carrelet *plaice (fish)*
carte *menu*
carte des vins *wine list*
casse-croûte *snacks*
cassis *black currant*
cassoulet *bean, pork and duck casserole*
céleri/céleri rave *celeriac*
céleri en branches *celery*
cèpe *cep (mushroom)*
cerise *cherry*
cerises à l'eau de vie *cherries in brandy*
cervelle *brains*
chabichou *goat's and cow's milk cheese*
chablis *dry white wine from Burgundy*
champignon *mushroom*
champignon de Paris *white button mushroom*
chanterelle *chanterelle (mushroom)*
chantilly *whipped cream*
charcuterie *sausages, ham and pâtés; pork products*
charlotte *dessert with fruit, cream, and cookies*
chausson aux pommes *apple turnover*
cheval *horse*
chèvre *goat's cheese*
chevreuil *venison*
chicorée *endive*
chocolat chaud *hot chocolate*
chocolat glacé *iced chocolate*
chou *cabbage*
chou à la crème *cream puff*
choucroute *sauerkraut with sausages and ham*
chou-fleur *cauliflower*
chou rouge *red cabbage*

choux de Bruxelles
Brussels sprouts
cidre *hard cider*
cidre doux *sweet cider*
citron *lemon*
citron pressé *fresh
lemonade*
civet de lièvre *stewed hare*
clafoutis *baked batter
pudding with fruit*
cochon de lait
suckling pig
cocktail de crevettes
shrimp cocktail
cœur *heart*
coing *quince*
colin *hake (fish)*
compote *stewed fruit*
comté *hard cheese from
the Jura*
concombre *cucumber*
confit de canard *duck
preserved in fat*
confit d'oie *goose
preserved in fat*
confiture *jam*
congre *conger eel*
consommé *clear meat or
chicken soup*
coq au vin *chicken in
red wine*
coque *cockle*
coquelet *cockerel*
coquilles Saint-Jacques
scallops in cream sauce
côte de porc *pork chop*
côtelette *chop*
cotriade bretonne *fish
soup from Brittany*
coulommiers *rich, soft
cheese*
court-bouillon *stock*
crabe *crab*
crème *cream; creamy
sauce or dessert; white
(coffee)*
crème à la vanille *vanilla
custard*
crème anglaise *custard*
crème chantilly
whipped cream
crème d'asperges *cream
of asparagus soup*
crème de bolets *cream of
mushroom soup*
crème de volaille *cream
of chicken soup*
crème d'huîtres *cream
of oyster soup*
crème fouettée *whipped
cream*
crème pâtissière *rich,
creamy custard*
crème renversée *set
custard*
crème vichyssoise *cold
leek and potato soup*
crêpe *crêpe*
crêpe à la crème de
marron *crêpe with
chestnut cream*

crêpe à l'œuf *crêpe with
fried egg*
crêpe de froment *wheat
crêpe*
crêpes Suzette *crêpes
flambéed with orange
sauce*
crépinette *small sausage
patty wrapped in fat*
cresson *cress*
crevette grise *shrimp*
crevette rose *shrimp*
croque-madame *grilled
cheese and ham sandwich
with a fried egg*
croque-monsieur *grilled
cheese and ham sandwich*
crottin de Chavignol
small goat's cheese
crustacés *shellfish*
cuisses de grenouille
frogs' legs

D

dartois *pastry with jam*
dégustation *wine-tasting*
digestif *liqueur*
dinde *turkey*
doux *sweet*

E

eau minérale gazeuse
sparkling mineral water
eau minérale plate *still
mineral water*
échalote *shallot*
écrevisse *freshwater
crayfish*
endive *chicory*
en papillote *baked in foil
or paper*
entrecôte *rib steak*
entrecôte au poivre
peppered rib steak
entrecôte maître d'hôtel
*steak with butter and
parsley*
entrée *appetizer*
entremets *dessert*
épaule d'agneau farcie
stuffed shoulder of lamb
épinards en branches
leaf spinach
escalope de veau
milanaise *veal escalope
with tomato sauce*
escalope panée *breaded
escalope*
escargot *snail*
estouffade de bœuf
beef casserole
estragon *tarragon*

F

faisan *pheasant*
farci *stuffed*
fenouil *fennel*
filet *fillet*

filet de bœuf Rossini
fillet of beef with foie gras
filet de perche *perch fillet*
fine *fine brandy*
flageolets *kidney beans*
flan *custard tart*
foie de veau *veal liver*
foie gras *goose or duck
liver preserve*
foies de volaille *chicken
livers*
fonds d'artichaut
artichoke hearts
fondue bourguignonne
meat fondue
fondue savoyarde
cheese fondue
fraise *strawberry*
fraise des bois *wild
strawberry*
framboise *raspberry*
frisée *curly lettuce*
frit *deep-fried*
frites *French fries*
fromage *cheese*
fromage blanc *cream
cheese*
fromage de chèvre *goat's
cheese*
fruits de mer *seafood*

G

galette *round, flat cake or
savory whole-wheat crêpe*
garni *with potatoes and
vegetables*
gâteau *cake*
gaufre *wafer; waffle*
gelée *gelatin*
Gewurztraminer *dry
white wine from Alsace*
gibier *game*
gigot d'agneau *leg of
lamb*
girolle *chanterelle
(mushroom)*
glace *ice cream*
goujon *gudgeon (fish)*
gratin *dish baked with
milk, cheese, and cream*
gratin dauphinois *sliced
potatoes baked in milk,
cream, and cheese*
gratinée *baked onion soup*
grillé *grilled*
grondin *gurnard (fish)*
groseille rouge *red
currant*

H

hachis parmentier
shepherd's pie
hareng mariné *marinated
herring*
haricots *beans*
haricots blancs *haricot
beans*
haricots verts *green beans*
homard *lobster*

hors-d'œuvre *appetizer*
huître *oyster*

I, J

îles flottantes *"floating islands"* (soft meringue on custard)
infusion *herb tea*
jambon *ham*
jambon de Bayonne *smoked and cured ham*
julienne *soup with chopped vegetables*
jus de fruits *fruit juice*
jus de pomme *apple juice*
jus d'orange *orange juice*

K, L

kir *white wine with black-currant liqueur*
kirsch *cherry brandy*
lait *milk*
laitue *lettuce*
langouste *saltwater crayfish*
langoustine *Dublin Bay prawn or Danish lobster*
lapereau *young rabbit*
lapin *rabbit*
lapin de garenne *wild rabbit*
lard *bacon*
légume *vegetable*
lentilles *lentils*
lièvre *hare*
limande *lemon sole*
livarot *strong, soft cheese from northern France*
longe *loin*
lotte *monkfish*
loup au fenouil *bass with fennel*

M

macédoine de légumes *mixed vegetables*
mache *corn salad (leafy vegetable)*
mangue *mango*
maquereau *mackerel*
marc *grape brandy*
marcassin *young boar*
marchand de vin *in red wine sauce*
marron *chestnut*
massepain *marzipan*
menthe *peppermint*
menthe à l'eau *mint cordial with water*
menu du jour *today's menu*
menu gastronomique *gourmet menu*
menu touristique *tourist menu*
merlan *whiting (fish)*
millefeuille *custard pastry*
millésime *vintage*

morille *morel (mushroom)*
morue *cod*
moules *mussels*
moules marinière *mussels in white wine*
mousseux *sparkling*
moutarde *mustard*
mouton *mutton*
mulet *mullet (fish)*
munster *strong cheese*
mûre *blackberry*
Muscadet *dry white wine*
myrtille *bilberry*

N

nature *plain*
navarin *mutton stew with vegetables*
navet *turnip*
noisette *hazelnut*
noisette d'agneau *medallion of lamb*
noix *nuts, walnuts*
nouilles *noodles*

O

œuf à la coque *boiled egg*
œuf dur *hard-boiled egg*
œuf mollet *soft-boiled egg*
œuf poché *poached egg*
œufs brouillés *scrambled eggs*
œuf sur le plat *fried egg*
oie *goose*
oignon *onion*
omelette au naturel *plain omelet*
omelette aux fines herbes *herb omelet*
omelette paysanne *omelet with potatoes and bacon*
orange pressée *fresh orange juice*
oseille *sorrel*
oursin *sea urchin*

P

pain *bread*
pain au chocolat *chocolate croissant*
palette de porc *shoulder of pork*
palourde *clam*
pamplemousse *grapefruit*
pastis *anise-flavored alcoholic drink*
pâté de canard *duck pâté*
pâté de foie de volaille *chicken liver pâté*
pâte feuilletée *puff pastry*
pâtes *pasta*
pêche *peach*
perdreau *young partridge*
perdrix *partridge*
petite friture *whitebait*

petit pain *roll*
petit pois *peas*
petits fours *small pastries*
petit suisse *cream cheese*
pied de porc *pig's feet*
pigeonneau *young pigeon*
pignatelle *cheese fritter*
pilaf de mouton *rice dish with mutton*
pintade *guinea fowl*
piperade *dish of egg, tomatoes, and peppers*
pissaladière *Provençal dish similar to pizza*
pistache *pistachio*
plat du jour *dish of the day*
plateau de fromages *cheese board*
pochouse *fish casserole with white wine*
poire *pear*
poireau *leek*
poisson *fish*
poivre *pepper*
poivron *red/green pepper*
pomme *apple*
pomme de terre *potato*
pommes de terre à l'anglaise *boiled potatoes*
pommes de terre en robe de chambre/des champs *baked potatoes*
pommes de terre sautées *fried potatoes*
pommes frites *French fries*
pommes paille *finely cut French fries*
pommes vapeur *steamed potatoes*
porc *pork*
potage *soup*
potage bilibi *fish and oyster soup*
potage Crécy *carrot and rice soup*
potage cressonnière *watercress soup*
potage Esaü *lentil soup*
potage parmentier *leek and potato soup*
potage printanier *vegetable soup*
potage Saint-Germain *split pea soup*
potage velouté *creamy soup*
pot-au-feu *beef and vegetable stew*
potée *vegetable and meat stew*
Pouilly-Fuissé *dry white wine from Burgundy*
poule au pot *chicken and vegetable stew*
poulet basquaise *chicken with ratatouille*
poulet chasseur *chicken with mushrooms and white wine*

poulet créole *chicken in white sauce with rice*
poulet rôti *roast chicken*
praire *clam*
provençale *with tomatoes, garlic and herbs*
prune *plum*
pruneau *prune*
pudding *plum pudding*
purée *mashed potatoes*

Q

quenelle *meat or fish dumpling*
queue de bœuf *oxtail*
quiche lorraine *egg, bacon, and cream quiche*

R

raclette *Swiss dish of melted cheese*
radis *radish*
ragoût *stew*
raie *skate* (fish)
raie au beurre noir *skate fried in butter*
raifort *horseradish*
raisin *grape*
râpé *grated*
rascasse *scorpion fish*
ratatouille *stew of peppers, zucchini, eggplant, and tomatoes*
ravigote *herb dressing*
reblochon *strong cheese from Savoy*
rémoulade *mayonnaise dressing with herbs, mustard, and capers*
rigotte *small goat's cheese from Lyon*
rillettes *preserved pork or goose meat*
ris de veau *veal sweetbread*
riz *rice*
riz pilaf *spicy rice with meat or seafood*
rognon *kidney*
roquefort *blue cheese*
rôti *roasted meat*
rouget *mullet*

S

sabayon *zabaglione (whipped egg yolk in Marsala wine)*
sablé *shortbread*
saignant *rare*
saint-honoré *cream puff cake*
saint-marcellin *goat's cheese*
salade composée *mixed salad*
salade russe *diced vegetables in mayonnaise*
salade verte *green salad*

salmis *game stew*
salsifis *oyster plant, salsify*
sanglier *wild boar*
sauce aurore *white sauce with tomato purée*
sauce béarnaise *thick sauce of eggs and butter*
sauce blanche *white sauce*
sauce gribiche *dressing with hard-boiled eggs*
sauce hollandaise *rich sauce of eggs, butter and vinegar, served with fish*
sauce Madère *Madeira sauce*
sauce matelote *wine sauce*
sauce Mornay *béchamel sauce with cheese*
sauce mousseline *hollandaise sauce with cream*
sauce poulette *sauce of mushrooms and egg yolks*
sauce ravigote *dressing with shallots and herbs*
sauce suprême *creamy sauce*
sauce tartare *mayonnaise with herbs and pickles*
sauce velouté *white sauce with egg yolks and cream*
sauce vinot *wine sauce*
saucisse *sausage*
saucisse de Francfort *frankfurter*
saucisse de Strasbourg *beef sausage*
saucisson *salami*
saumon *salmon*
saumon fumé *smoked salmon*
sauternes *sweet white wine*
savarin *rum baba*
sec *dry*
seiche *cuttlefish*
sel *salt*
service (non) compris *service (not) included*
service 12% inclus *12% service charge included*
sole bonne femme *sole in white wine and mushrooms*
sole meunière *floured sole fried in butter*
soupe *soup*
soupe au pistou *thick vegetable soup with basil*
steak au poivre *peppered steak*
steak frites *steak and fries*
steak haché *ground beef*
steak tartare *raw ground beef with a raw egg*
sucre *sugar*

suprême de volaille *chicken in cream sauce*

T

tanche *tench* (fish)
tarte aux fraises *strawberry tart*
tarte aux pommes *apple tart*
tarte frangipane *almond cream tart*
tartelette *small tart*
tarte Tatin *baked apple dish*
tartine *bread and butter*
tendrons de veau *breast of veal*
terrine *pâté*
tête de veau *calf's head*
thé *tea*
thé à la menthe *mint tea*
thé au lait *tea with milk*
thé citron *lemon tea*
thon *tuna*
tomates farcies *stuffed tomatoes*
tome de Savoie *white cheese from Savoy*
tournedos *round beef steak*
tourte *covered pie*
tourteau *type of crab*
tripes à la mode de Caen *tripe in spicy vegetable sauce*
truite au bleu *poached trout*
truite aux amandes *trout with almonds*
truite meunière *trout in flour and fried in butter*

V, Y

vacherin *strong, soft cheese from the Jura*
vacherin glacé *ice cream meringue*
veau *veal*
velouté de tomate *cream of tomato soup*
vermicelle *vermicelli (very fine pasta)*
viande *meat*
vin *wine*
vinaigrette *oil and vinegar dressing*
vin blanc *white wine*
vin de pays *local wine*
vin de table *table wine*
vin rosé *rosé wine*
vin rouge *red wine*
volaille *poultry*
VSOP *mature brandy*
yaourt *yogurt*

Dictionary
English to French

The gender of a singular French noun is indicated by the word for *the*: **le** and **la** (masculine and feminine). If these are abbreviated to **l'** in front of a vowel or the letter "h," or if the noun is plural, indicated by **les**, then the gender is indicated by the abbreviations "(m)" or "(f)." French adjectives (adj) vary according to the gender and number of the word they describe; the masculine form is shown here. In most cases, you add an **-e** to the masculine form to make it feminine. Certain endings use a different rule: masculine adjectives that end in **-x** adopt an **-se** ending in the feminine form, while those that end in **-ien** change to **-ienne**. Some feminine adjectives that do not follow these rules are shown here and follow the abbreviation "(fem)." For the plural form, a (silent) **-s** is usually added.

A

a un/une
about: about sixteen environ seize
accelerator l'accélérateur (m)
accident l'accident (m)
accommodation l'hébergement (m)
accountant le/la comptable
ache la douleur
adapter (plug) la prise multiple; (voltage); l'adaptateur (m)
address l'adresse (f)
adhesive l'adhésif (m)
admission charge le prix d'entrée
advance l'avance (f)
after après
afternoon l'après-midi (m)
aftershave l'après-rasage (m)
again de nouveau
against contre
agenda l'ordre du jour (m)
agent l'agent (m)
AIDS SIDA
air l'air (m)
air conditioning la climatisation
aircraft l'avion (m)
airline la compagnie aérienne
air mail par avion
air mattress le matelas pneumatique
airport l'aéroport (m)

airport bus la navette (pour l'aéroport)
aisle (supermarket) rayon
alarm clock le réveil
alcohol l'alcool (m)
Algeria l'Algérie (f)
Algerian algérien(ne)
all tout; *all the streets* toutes les rues; *that's all* c'est tout
allergic allergique
almost presque
alone seul
Alps les Alpes (f)
already déjà
always toujours
am: I am je suis
ambulance l'ambulance (f)
America l'Amérique (f)
American américain(e)
and et
Andorra Andorre
ankle la cheville
another (different) un/une autre; *another coffee, please* encore un café, s'il vous plaît
answering machine le réponder
antifreeze l'antigel (m)
antique shop le magasin d'antiquités; l'antiquaire (m)
antiseptic l'antiseptique (m)
apartment l'appartement (m)
aperitif l'apéritif (m)
appetite l'appétit (m)
appetizers les entrées (f)

apple la pomme
application form le formulaire de demande
appointment le rendez-vous
apricot l'abricot (m)
April avril
architecture l'architecture (f)
are: you are (singular informal) tu es; *we are* nous sommes; (plural; singular formal) vous êtes; *they are* ils/elles sont
arm le bras
armchair le fauteuil
arrival l'arrivée (f)
arrive arriver
art l'art (m)
art gallery le musée d'art; la galerie d'art
artist l'artiste (m)
as: as soon as possible dès que possible
ashtray le cendrier
asleep endormi; *he's asleep* il dort
aspirin l'aspirine (f)
associate professor le maître de conférences
asthmatic asthmatique
at: at the post office à la poste; *at the café* au café; *at 3 o'clock* à 3 heures
ATM le distributeur automatique
attic le grenier
attractive attirant
August août
aunt la tante
Australia l'Australie (f)

Australian australien(ne)

automatic automatique

autumn l'automne (m)

avocado l'avocat (m)

away: is it far away? est-ce que c'est loin?; *go away!* allez-vous en!

awful affreux

ax la hache

axle l'essieu (m)

B

baby le bébé

baby carriage le landau

baby wipes les lingettes (f)

back (not front) l'arrière (m); *(body)* le dos; *I'll come back tomorrow* je reviendrai demain

backpack le sac à dos

bacon le bacon; *bacon and eggs* des œufs au bacon

bad mauvais

baggage les bagages (m)

baggage check-in l'enregistrement des bagages (m)

baggage claim la réclamation de bagages

bait l'appât (m)

bake cuire

bakery la pâtisserie

balcony le balcon

bald chauve

ball (soccer, etc.) le ballon; *(tennis, etc.)* la balle

ballpoint pen le stylo-bille

banana la banane

band (musicians) le groupe

bandage le pansement, le bandage

bangs (hair) la frange

bank la banque

bank note le billet

bar le bar;

barbecue le barbecue

barber's le coiffeur

bargain la affaire

basement le sous-sol

basin (sink) le lavabo

basket le panier

bath le bain; *(bathtub)* la baignoire; *to take a bath* prendre un bain

bathroom la salle de bains

battery (car) la batterie; *(flashlight)* la pile

be être

beach la plage

beans les haricots (m)

beard la barbe

beautiful beau, *(fem)* belle

because parce que

bed le lit

bed linen les draps (m)

bedroom la chambre

beef le bœuf

beer la bière

before avant

beginner le débutant, la débutante

beginners' slope la piste pour débutants

behind derrière

beige beige

Belgian belge

Belgium la Belgique

bell (church) la cloche; *(door)* la sonnette

below ... sous ...

belt la ceinture

beside à côté de

best: the best le meilleur

better mieux

between ... entre ...

bicycle la bicyclette, le vélo

big grand

bill l'addition (f)

bird l'oiseau (m)

birthday l'anniversaire (m); *happy birthday!* joyeux anniversaire!

bite (by dog) la morsure; *(by snake, insect)* la piqûre; *(verb: dog)* mordre; *(insect, snake)* piquer

bitter amer

black noir

blackberry la mûre

black currant le cassis

blanket la couverture

bleach l'eau de Javel (f); *(verb)* décolorer

blind (cannot see) aveugle; *(window)* le store

blister l'ampoule (f)

blizzard la tempête de neige

blond (adj) blond

blood le sang

blood test la prise de sang

blouse le chemisier

blue bleu

boarding pass la carte d'embarquement

boat le bateau; *(smaller)* la barque

body le corps

boil (verb) bouillir

boiled bouilli

boiler le chauffe-eau

bolt (on door) le verrou; verrouiller *(verb)*

bone l'os (m); *(fish)* l'arête (f)

book le livre; réserver *(verb)*

bookstore la librairie

boot (footwear) la botte

border la frontière

boring ennuyeux

born: I was born in ... je suis né(e) en ...

both les deux; *both of them* tous les deux; *both of us* nous deux; *both large and small* grand et petit à la fois

bottle la bouteille

bottle opener le décapsuleur, l'ouvre-bouteille (m)

bottom le fond; *(part of body)* le derrière

bowl le bol; *(animal)* la gamelle

box la boîte

box office (theater, etc.) le bureau de location

boy le garçon

boyfriend le petit ami

bra le soutien-gorge

bracelet le bracelet

brake le frein; *(verb)* freiner

branch la branche

brandy le cognac

bread le pain

bread shop la boulangerie

breakdown (car) la panne; *(nervous)* la dépression; *My car has broken down* (car) je suis tombé en panne

breakfast le petit déjeuner

breathe respirer

bricklayer le maçon

bridge le pont

briefcase l'attaché-case (m)

British britannique

Brittany la Bretagne

brochure la brochure

broken cassé; *broken leg* la jambe cassée; *broken down* en panne

brooch la broche

brother le frère

brown marron

bruise le bleu

brush la brosse; *(paintbrush)* le pinceau; *(broom)* le balai; *(verb)* brosser

Brussels Bruxelles

bucket le seau

budget le budget

builder le constructeur

building le bâtiment
bumper le pare-chocs
bunker le bunker
burglary
le cambriolage
burn la brûlure;(verb)
brûler
bus le bus
business
les affaires (f);
*it's none of your
business* cela ne
vous regarde pas
business card la carte
de visite
bus station la gare
routière
bus stop
l'arrêt de bus (m)
busy (occupied)
occupé; (street)
animé
but mais
butcher's la boucherie
butter le beurre
button le bouton
buy acheter
by: by the window
près de la fenêtre;
by Friday d'ici
vendredi; *by myself*
tout seul; *written by*
écrit par

C

cabbage le chou
cabinet le placard
cable car le
téléphérique
cable TV
la télé câblée
café le café
cage la cage
cake le gâteau
calculator
la calculette
call: what's it called?
comment est-ce que
ça s'appelle?
camcorder
le caméscope
camera
l'appareil-photo (m)
camper van
le camping-car
campfire le feu de
camp
campground le terrain
de camping
campsite l'emplacement
(m)
cam shaft l'arbre à
cames (m)
can (vessel) la boîte
de conserve; (to be
able) pouvoir; *can I
have …?* Je peux avoir
…?; *can you …?* Vous
pouvez …?
Canada le Canada

Canadian canadien(ne)
canal le canal
candle la bougie
canoe le canoë
can opener
l'ouvre-boîte (m)
candy le bonbon
cap (hat) la casquette;
(bottle) la capsule
car la voiture; (train)
la voiture, le wagon
caravan la caravane
carburetor
le carburateur
card la carte
careful prudent; *careful!*
attention!; *be careful!*
soyez prudent!
caretaker
le/la concierge
carpenter
le charpentier
carpet le tapis
carrot la carotte
car seat (for a baby)
le siège pour bébé
cart le chariot
case la valise
cash l'argent (m);
to pay cash payer
en liquide
cashier le guichet
cassette la cassette
cassette player le lecteur
de cassettes
castle le château
cat le chat
cathedral
la cathédrale
cauliflower le chou-fleur
cave la grotte
CD le disque compact
ceiling le plafond
cell phone le téléphone
portable
cellar la cave
cemetery le cimetière
center le centre
central heating le
chauffage central
certificate le certificat
chair la chaise
change (money) la
monnaie; (verb:
money) changer;
(clothes) se changer
Channel la Manche
Channel Islands les îles
Anglo-Normandes
Channel Tunnel le
tunnel sous la Manche
charger le chargeur
cheap bon marché, pas
cher
check-in
l'enregistrement (m)
check in faire enregistrer
ses bagages
checkout
(supermarket) la
caisse

cheers! (toast) santé!
cheese le fromage
cheese shop la
fromagerie
check le chèque
checkbook le carnet
de chèques
cherry la cerise
chess les échecs (m)
chest la poitrine
chest of drawers la
commode
chicken le poulet
child l'enfant (m)
children
les enfants (m)
children's ward le
service de pédiatrie
chimney la cheminée
china la porcelaine
chips les chips (f)
chocolate le chocolat;
a box of chocolates
la boîte de chocolats;
chocolate bar la
tablette de chocolat
chop (food) la
côtelette; couper
(verb: cut)
church l'église (f)
cigar le cigare
cigarette la cigarette
city la ville
class la classe
classical music la
musique classique
clean (adj) propre
cleaner la femme de
ménages
clear clair
clock l'horloge (f),
la pendule
close près (near);
étouffant (stuffy);
fermer (verb)
closed fermé
clothes
les vêtements (m)
clubs (cards) trèfle
clutch
l'embrayage (m)
coat le manteau
coat hanger le cintre
cockroach le cafard
cocktail party
le cocktail
coffee le café; *coffee with
milk* café crème
coin la pièce
cold (illness) le rhume;
froid (adj)
collar le col, le collier
collection (stamps,
etc.) la collection;
color la couleur
color film la pellicule
couleur
comb le peigne;
peigner (verb)
come venir; *I come from
…* je viens de …; *we*

came last week nous sommes arrivés la semaine dernière
comforter la couette
company la compagnie
compartment le compartiment
complicated compliqué
computer l'ordinateur (m)
computer games les jeux vidéos (m)
concert le concert
conditioner (hair) le baume après-shampooing
condom le préservatif
conductor (orchestra) le chef d'orchestre
confectioner le confiseur
conference la conférence
conference room la salle de conférences
congratulations! félicitations!
consulate le consulat
consultant consultant(e)
contact lenses les verres de contact (f)
contraceptive le contraceptif
cook le cuisinier; faire la cuisine (verb)
cookie le biscuit
cooking utensils les utensiles de cuisine (f)
cool frais, (fem) fraîche
cork le bouchon
corkscrew le tire-bouchon
corner le coin
corridor le couloir
Corsica la Corse
Corsican corse
cosmetics les produits de beauté (m)
cost (verb) coûter; *how much does it cost?* combien ça coûte?
cotton le coton
cotton balls le coton hydrophile
cough la toux; tousser (verb)
countertop le plan de travail
country (state) le pays; (not town) la campagne
cousin le cousin
crab le crabe
cramp la crampe
crayfish (freshwater) l'écrevisse (f); (saltwater) la langouste

cream la crème
credit card la carte de crédit
crêpe la crêpe
crib le lit d'enfant
cross (verb) traverser
crowded bondé
cruise la croisière
crutches les béquilles (f)
cry (weep) pleurer; (shout) crier
cucumber le concombre
cufflinks les boutons de manchette (m)
cup la tasse
curlers les rouleaux (m)
curls les boucles (f)
current le courant
curry le curry
curtain le rideau
customs la douane
cut la coupure;(verb) couper
cycling le vélo

D

dad papa
dairy products les produits laitiers (m)
dance la danse;(verb) danser
dangerous dangereux
dark foncé; *dark blue* bleu foncé
daughter la fille
day le jour
dead mort
deaf sourd
dear cher
debit card la carte bancaire
December décembre
deck of cards le jeu de cartes
decorator le décorateur
deep profond
delay le retard
deliberately exprès
delicatessen la charcuterie
delivery la livraison
dentist le/la dentiste
dentures le dentier
deny nier
deodorant le déodorant
department la département
department store le grand magasin
departures (airport, etc.) le départ
designer le designer
desk le bureau
desserts les desserts (m)
develop développer

diabetic diabétique
diamond (jewel) le diamant
diamonds (cards) carreau
diaper la couche
diarrhea la diarrhée
dictionary le dictionnaire
die mourir
diesel le diesel; le gazoile
different différent; *that's different* c'est différent; *I'd like a different one* j'en voudrais un autre
difficult difficile
dining room la salle à manger
dinner le dîner
dinner party le dîner
directory (telephone) l'annuaire (m); les reseignments (m)
disabled handicapé
disco le discothèque
discount la réduction
dish cloth le torchon
dishwasher le lave-vaiselle
dishwashing liquid le produit pour la vaisselle
disposable diapers les couches à jeter (f)
distributor (car) le delco
dive (verb) plonger
diving board le plongeoir
divorced divorcé
do faire; *how do you do?* comment allez-vous?
dock le quai
doctor le docteur; médecin
document le document
dog le chien
doll la poupée
dollar le dollar
door (building) la porte; (car) la portière
double room la chambre pour deux personnes
doughnut le beignet
down en bas
downtown le centre-ville
drawer le tiroir
dress la robe
drink la boisson; (verb) boire; *would you like a drink?* vous voulez boire quelque chose?
drinking water l'eau potable (f)

drive (verb: car)
conduire
driver le conducteur
driveway le passage
driver's license
le permis de conduire
drops les goutes (f)
drunk soûl, ivre
dry sec, (fem) sèche
dry-cleaner
le pressing
during pendant
duster le chiffon à
poussière
duty-free hors-taxe

E

each (every) chaque;
two euros each deux
euros pièce
ear l'oreille (f)
early tôt
earrings les boucles
d'oreille (f)
east l'est (m)
easy facile
eat manger
egg l'œuf (m)
eight huit
eighteen dix-huit
eighty quatre-vingt
either: either of them
n'importe lequel;
either … or … soit …
soit …
elastic élastique
elastic band
l'élastique (m)
elbow le coude
electric électrique
electrician
électricien(ne)
electricity
l'électricité (f)
elevator l'ascenseur (m)
eleven onze
else: something else
autre chose; *someone
else* quelqu'un
d'autre; *somewhere
else* ailleurs
email l'email (m),
le message,
la messagerie
électronique
email address l'adresse
électronique (f)
embarrassing gênant
embassy
l'ambassade (f)
embroidery la broderie
emerald
l'émeraude (f)
emergency l'urgence (f)
emergency exit la sortie
de secours
*emergency
room* la salle des
urgences
empty vide

end la fin
engaged (couple)
fiancé
engine (car) le moteur;
(train) la locomotive
engineer
l'ingénieur (m)
engineering
l'ingénierie (f)
England
l'Angleterre (f)
English anglais(e)
enlargement
l'agrandissement (m)
enough assez
entertainment le
divertissement
entrance l'entrée (f)
envelope
l'enveloppe (f)
epileptic épileptique
eraser la gomme
escalator l'escalier
roulant (m)
especially
particulièrement
estimate
l'estimation (f)
evening le soir
every chaque
everyone tout le monde
everything tout
everywhere partout
example l'exemple
(m); *for example*
par exemple
excellent excellent
excess baggage
l'excédent de
bagages (m)
exchange (verb)
échanger
exchange rate le taux
de change
excursion
l'excursion (f)
excuse me! pardon!
executive (in
company) cadre (m)
exhaust (car) le pot
d'echappement
exhibition
l'exposition (f)
exit la sortie
expensive cher
extension lead la
rallonge
exterior
l'extérieure (m)
eye l'œil (m)
eyebrow le sourcil
eyes les yeux (m)

F

face le visage
faint vague; *to faint*
evanouir
fair la foire; (just)
juste; *it's not fair* ce
n'est pas juste

fan (ventilator) le
ventilateur;
(enthusiast) le/la
fan
fan belt la courroie du
ventilateur
fantastic fantastique
far loin; *how far is it to
…?* est-ce que … est
loin d'ici?
fare le prix du billet
farm la ferme
farmer le fermier
fashion la mode
fast rapide
fat (of person) gros,
(fem) grosse; (on
meat, etc.) le gras
father le père
fax le fax; (verb:
document) toucher;
fax machine le fax
February fevrier
feel (touch) toucher;
I feel hot j'ai chaud;
I feel like … j'ai envie
de …; *I don't feel
well* je ne me sens
pas bien
feet les pieds (m)
felt-tip pen le feutre
ferry (small) le bac;
(large) le ferry
fever la fièvre
fiancé le fiancé
fiancée la fiancée
field le champ;
(academic)
secteur (m)
fifteen quinze
fifty cinquante
fig la figue
figures
les chiffres (m)
filling (in tooth) le
plombage; (in
sandwich, cake)
la garniture
film le film
filter paper le papier
filtre
finger le doigt
fire le feu; (blaze)
l'incendie (m)
fire extinguisher
l'extincteur (m)
fireplace la cheminée
fireworks le feu
d'artifice
first premier
first aid les premiers
soins (m)
first class première
classe
first floor le premier
étage
first name le prénom
fish le poisson
fishing la pêche;
to go fishing aller à
la pêche

fishing rod la canne à pêche
fishmonger la poissonnerie
five cinq
flag le drapeau
flash (camera) le flash
flashlight la lampe de poche
flat (level) plat
flat tire le pneu crevé
flavor le goût
flea la puce
flight le vol
flight attendant l'hôtesse de l'air (f)
flip-flops les tongs (f)
flippers les palmes (f)
floor (ground) le plancher; (storey) l'étage (m)
florist la fleuriste
flour la farine
flower la fleur
flowerbed le parterre de fleurs
flute la flûte
fly (insect) la mouche; (verb: of plane, etc.) voler; (of person) prendre l'avion
fog le brouillard
folk music la musique folklorique
food la nourriture
food poisoning l'intoxication alimentaire (f)
foot le pied
for pour; *for me* pour moi; *what for?* pour quoi faire?; *for a week* pour une semaine
foreigner l'étranger (m)
forest la forêt
forget oublier
fork la fourchette
forty quarante
fountain pen le stylo-plume
four quatre
fourteen quatorze
fourth quatrième
France la France
free (no cost) gratuit; (at liberty) libre
freezer le congélateur
French français(e)
French fries les frites (f)
Friday vendredi
fried frit
friend l'ami(e)
friendly amical, gentil
front: in front devant
frost le gel
frozen foods les produits surgelés (m)
fruit le fruit

fruit juice le jus de fruit
fry frire
frying pan la poêle
full complet; *I'm full!* j'ai l'estomac bien rempli!
full board la pension complète
funny drôle
furnished meublé
furniture les meubles (m)

G

garage le garage
garbage les ordures (f); les détritus (m)
garbage can la poubelle
garden le jardin
garden center la jardinerie
garlic l'ail (m)
gas le gaz
gas-permeable lenses les lentilles semi-souples (f)
gas station la station-service
gasoline l'essence (f)
gate le portail, la grille; (at airport) la porte d'embarquement
gay homosexuel
gear (car) la vitesse
gearbox la boîte de vitesses
gearshift le levier de vitesse
gel le gel
German allemand(e)
Germany l'Allemagne (f)
get (fetch) aller chercher; *do you have ...?* avez-vous ...?; *to take the train* prendre le train; *get back: we get back tomorrow* nous rentrons demain; *to get something back* récupérer quelque chose
get in entrer; (arrive) arriver
get off (bus, etc.) descendre
get on (bus, etc.) monter
get out sortir
get up se lever
gift le cadeau
gin le gin
ginger le gingembre
girl (child) la fille; (young woman) la jeune fille
girlfriend la petite amie
give donner

glad heureux
glass le verre
glasses les lunettes (f)
gloves les gants (m)
glue la colle
go aller
gold l'or (m)
golf le golf
golf course le parcours de golf
good bon, (fem) bonne; *good!* bien!
goodbye au revoir
good evening bonsoir
government le gouvernement
granddaughter la petite-fille
grandfather le grand-père
grandmother la grand-mère
grandparents les grands-parents (m)
grandson le petit-fils
grapes les raisins (m)
grass l'herbe (f)
gray gris
Great Britain la Grande-Bretagne
green vert
grill le gril
grilled grillé(e)
grocery store l'épicerie (f)
ground floor le rez-de-chaussée
groundsheet le tapis de sol
guarantee la garantie; (verb) garantir
guard (train) le chef de train
guest l'invitée
guide le/la guide
guide book le guide
guitar la guitare
gun (rifle) le fusil; (pistol) le pistolet
gutter la gouttière
gym le centre sportif

H

hair les cheveux (m); *long/short hair* les cheveux longs/courts
haircut la coupe (de cheveux)
hairdresser le coiffeur
hairdryer le sèche-cheveux
hairspray la laque
half demi; *half an hour* une demi-heure
half-board la demi-pension
ham le jambon
hamburger le hamburger

hammer le marteau
hamster le hamster
hand la main
hand luggage le bagage à main
handbag le sac à main
handbrake le frein à main
handkerchief le mouchoir
handle (door) la poignée
handsome beau
hangover la gueule de bois
happy heureux
harbor le port
hard dur; (difficult) difficile
hard lenses les lentilles rigides (f)
hardware store la quincaillerie
hat le chapeau
have avoir; *do you have ...?* avez-vous ...?
hay fever le rhume des foins
he il
head la tête
headache le mal à la tête
headlights les phares (m)
headphones les écouteurs (m)
headquarters le siège social
hear entendre
hearing aid l'appareil acoustique
heart le cœur
heart condition le problème au cœur
hearts (cards) cœurs
heater le radiateur
heating le chauffage
heavy lourd
hedge la haie
heel le talon
hello bonjour
help l'aide (f); (verb) aider
hepatitis l'hépatite (f)
her: it's for her c'est pour elle; *give it to her* donnez-le lui
her: her book son livre; *her house* sa maison; *her shoes* ses chaussures; *it's hers* c'est à elle
hi salut
high haut
highway l'autoroute (f)
highway code le code de la route
hiking la randonée
hill la colline
him: it's for him c'est pour lui; *give it to him* donnez-le lui

his: his book son livre; *his house* sa maison; *his shoes* ses chaussures; *it's his* c'est à lui
history l'histoire (f)
hitchhike faire de l'autostop
HIV-positive séropositif(ve)
hobby le passe-temps
home: at home (my home) chez moi; *he's at home* il est chez lui
homeopathy homéopathie
honest honnête
honey le miel
honeymoon la lune de miel
hood (car) le capot
horn (car) le klaxon; (animal) la corne
horrible horrible
hospital l'hôpital (m)
host l'hôte (m)
hostess l'hôtesse (f)
hot chaud
hotel l'hôtel (m)
hour l'heure (f)
house la maison
household products les produits entretien (m)
hovercraft l'aéroglisseur (m)
hoverport l'hoverport (m)
how? comment?
how much? combien?
hundred cent
hungry: I'm hungry j'ai faim
hurry: I'm in a hurry je suis pressé
husband le mari
hydrofoil l'hydrofoil (m)

I

I je
ice la glace
ice cream la glace
ice rink la patinoire
ice skates les patins à glace (m)
ice-skating: to go ice-skating aller patiner
identification la identification
if si
ignition l'allumage (m)
ill malade
immediately immédiatement
impossible impossible
in dans; *in France* en France
indigestion l'indigestion (f)
inexpensive bon marché, pas cher

infection l'infection (f)
information l'information (f)
injection la piqûre
injury la blessure
ink l'encre (f)
inn l'auberge (f)
inner tube la chambre à air
insect l'insecte (m)
insect repellent la crème anti-insecte
insomnia l'insomnie (f)
instant coffee le café soluble
insurance l'assurance (f)
interesting intéressant
Internet l'internet (m)
interpret interpréter
interpreter l'interprète (m)
invitation l'invitation (f)
invoice la facture
Ireland l'Irlande (f)
Irish irlandais(e)
iron ((for clothes) le fer à repasser; (verb) repasser
is: he/she is il/elle est; *it is* c'est
island l'île (f)
it il; elle
Italian italien(ne)
Italy l'Italie (f)
its son; sa; ses (see his)

J

jacket la veste
jam la confiture
January janvier
jeans les jeans (m)
jellyfish la méduse
jeweler la bijouterie
job le travail
jog (verb) faire du jogging; *to go for a jog* aller faire du jogging
jogging suit le survêtement
joke la plaisanterie
journey le voyage
July juillet
June juin
just: it's just arrived ça vient juste d'arriver; *I've just one left* il ne m'en reste qu'un

K

kerosene le pétrole
kettle la bouilloire
key la clé
keyboard le clavier
kidney le rein
kilo le kilo
kilometer le kilomètre
kind gentil

kitchen la cuisine
knee le genou
knife le couteau
knitting needle l'aiguille à tricoter (f)
know (fact) savoir; (person) connaître; *I don't know* je ne sais pas

L

label l'étiquette (f)
lace la dentelle; (of shoe) le lacet
lake le lac
lamb l'agneau (m)
lamp la lampe
lampshade l'abat-jour (m)
land la terre; (verb) atterrir
language la langue
laptop l'ordinateur portable (m)
large grand
last (final) dernier; *last week* la semaine dernière; *at last!* enfin!
last name le nom de famille
late tard; *the bus is late* le bus est en retard
later plus tard
laugh rire
laundromat la laverie automatique
laundry (place) la blanchisserie; (clothes) le linge
laundry detergent la lessive
law (subject) le droit
lawn la pelouse
lawnmower la tondeuse à gazon
lawyer avocat(e)
laxative le laxatif
lazy paresseux
lead la laisse
leaf la feuille
leaflet le dépliant
learn apprendre
leather le cuir
lecture hall l'amphithéâtre (m)
leek le poireaux
left (not right) la gauche; *there's nothing left* il ne reste plus rien
leg la jambe
lemon le citron
lemonade le citron pressé
length la longueur
lens (camera) l'objectif (m)
less moins
lesson la leçon
letter la lettre

lettuce la salade
library la bibliothèque
license le permis
license plate la plaque d'immatriculation
life la vie
light la lumière; (not heavy) léger; (not dark) clair
light bulb l'ampoule (f)
lighter le briquet
lighter fluid le gaz à briquet
light meter la cellule photoélectrique
like (verb) aimer: *I like swimming* j'aime nager; *I don't like* je n'aime pas; (similar to) comme
lime (fruit) le citron vert
lipstick le rouge à lèvres
liqueur la liqueur
list la liste
liter le litre
literature la litérature
litter les ordures (f)
little (small) petit; *it's a little big* c'est un peu trop grand; *just a little* juste un peu
liver le foie
living room le salon
lobster le homard
lollipop la sucette
long long, (fem) longue
lost property les objets trouvés (m)
loud fort; (color) criard
love l'amour (m), (verb) aimer
lover l'amant (m)
low bas
luck la chance; *good luck!* bonne chance!
luggage les bagages (m)
luggage lockers la consigne automatique
luggage rack le porte-bagages
lunch le déjeuner
Luxembourg le Luxembourg

M

mad fou, (fem) folle
magazine la revue
maid la femme de chambre
mail la poste; (verb) poster
mail carrier le facteur
mailbox la boîte à lettres
main courses les plats (m)
make faire
makeup le maquillage
man l'homme (m)

manager le directeur; le chef
many beaucoup; *not many* pas beaucoup
map la carte; (town map) le plan
March mars
margarine la margarine
market le marché
marmalade la marmelade d'oranges
married marié
mascara le mascara
mass (church) la messe
mast le mât
match (light) l'allumette (f); (sport) le match
material (cloth) le tissu
matter: it doesn't matter ça ne fait rien
mattress le matelas
May mai
maybe peut-être
me: it's me c'est moi; *it's for me* c'est pour moi; *give it to me* donnez-le-moi
meal le repas
mean: what does this mean? qu'est-ce que cela veut dire?
meat la viande
mechanic le mécanicien, le garagiste
medication les médicaments (m)
medicine le médicament; (subject) le médicine
Mediterranean la Méditerranée
meeting la réunion
melon le melon
menu la carte; *set menu* le menu
message le message
metro le métro
microwave le micro-ondes
middle le milieu
midnight minuit
milk le lait
mine: it's mine c'est à moi
mineral water l'eau minérale (f)
minute la minute
mirror le miroir; (car) le rétroviseur
Miss Mademoiselle
mistake l'erreur (f)
modem le modem
Monday lundi
money l'argent (m)
monitor (computer) le moniteur
month le mois
monument le monument
moon la lune

moped la mobylette
more plus; *more or less* plus ou moins
morning le matin; *in the morning* dans la matinée
mosquito le moustique
mother la mère
motorboat le bateau à moteur
motorcycle la moto
mountain la montagne
mountain bike le vélo tout terrain
mouse la souris
mousse (hair) la mousse
mouth la bouche
move bouger; (house) déménager; *don't move!* ne bougez pas!
movie theater le cinéma
Mr. Monsieur
Mrs. Madame
mug la tasse
museum le musée
mushroom le champignon
music la musique
musical instrument l'instrument de musique (m)
musician le musicien
mussels les moules (f)
must: I must je dois
mustache la moustache
mustard la moutarde
my: my book mon livre; *my house* ma maison; *my shoes* mes chaussures

N

nail (metal) le clou; (finger) l'ongle (m)
nail clippers la pince à ongles
nail file la lime à ongles
nail polish le vernis à ongles
name le nom; *what's your name* comment vous appelez-vous?
narrow étroit
near: near the door près de la porte
necessary nécessaire
neck le cou
necklace le collier
need (verb) avoir besoin de; *I need ...* j'ai besoin de ...; *there's no need* ce n'est pas nécessaire
needle l'aiguille (f)
negative (photo) le négatif
neither: neither of them ni l'un ni l'autre; *neither ... nor ...* ni ... ni ...
nephew le neveu
never jamais
new nouveau, (fem) nouvelle; neuf, (fem) neuve
news les nouvelles (f); (television) les informations (f)
newspaper le journal
newsstand le tabac; le tabac-journaux
next prochain; *next week* la semaine prochaine; *what next?* et puis quoi?
nice (place, etc.) joli; (person) sympathique
niece la nièce
night la nuit
nightclub la boîte de nuit
nightgown la chemise de nuit
nine neuf
nineteen dix-neuf
ninety quatre-vingt-dix
no (response) non; (not any) aucun
nobody personne
noisy bruyant
none aucun
noon midday
north le nord
nose le nez
not pas; *he's not ...* il n'est pas ...
notebook le carnet
notepad le bloc notes
nothing rien
novel le roman
November novembre
now maintenant
nowhere nulle part
nudist le nudiste
number (figure) le numéro; (amount) le nombre
nurse infirmier; (fem) infirmière
nut (fruit) la noix; (for bolt) l'écrou (m)

O

oars les rames (f)
occasionally de temps en temps
October octobre
of de
of course bien sûr
office le bureau
often souvent
oil l'huile (f)
ointment la pommade
OK d'accord
old vieux, (fem) vieille; *how old are you?* quel âge avez-vous?

olive l'olive (f)
omelet l'omelette (f)
on ... sur ...
one un/une
one-way ticket l'aller simple (m) *onion* l'oignon (m)
only seulement
open (adj) ouvert; (verb) ouvrir
opening times les heures d'ouverture (f)
operating room la salle d'opérations
operation l'opération (f)
operator (phone) l'opérateur (m)
opposite en face de
optician's l'opticien (m)
or ou
orange (fruit) l'orange (f); (color) orange
orange juice le jus d'orange
orchestra l'orchestre (m)
ordinary habituel
organ (music) l'orgue (m)
other: the other ... l'autre ...
our: our house notre maison; *our children* nos enfants; *it's ours* c'est à nous
out: he's out il n'est pas là
outside dehors
oven le four
over (above) au-dessus de; (more than) plus de; (finished) fini; *it's over the road* c'est de l'autre côté de la rue; *over there* là-bas
oyster l'huître (f)

P

package le paquet; (parcel) le colis
package le colis
packet le paquet
padlock le cadenas
page la page
pain la douleur
paint la peinture
painting la peinture
pair la paire
palace le palais
pale pâle, blême
pants le pantalon
panty hose les collants (m)
paper le papier; (newspaper) le journal
pardon? pardon?
parents les parents (m)

park le jardin public;
(verb) garer
parking lot le parking
part (in hair) la raie
party (celebration) la
fête, la soirée;
(group) le groupe;
(political) le parti
pass (in a car) doubler
passenger le passager
passport le passeport
passport control le
contrôle des passeports
password le mot de
passe
pasta les pâtes (f)
path le chemin,
l'allée (f)
pay payer
payment le paiement
peach la pêche
peanuts
les cacahuètes (f)
pear la poire
pearl la perle
peas les petits pois (m)
pedestrian le piéton
peg la pince à linge
pen le stylo
pencil le crayon
pencil sharpener le
taille-crayon
penknife le canif
pen pal le
correspondant
people les gens (m)
pepper (and salt) le
poivre; (red/green) le
poivron
peppermints les
bonbons à la
menthe (m)
per: per night par nuit
perfect parfait
perfume le parfum
perhaps peut-être
perm la permanente
pet passport le
passeport d'animaux
pets les animaux
(familiers) (m)
pharmacy la pharmacie
phone card la carte
téléphonique
photocopier le copieur
photograph la photo;
(verb) photographier
photographer le/la
photographe
phrasebook le guide
de conversation
piano le piano
pickpocket le pickpocket
pickup (mail) la levée
picnic le pique-nique
piece le morceau
pill le comprimé
pillow l'oreiller (m)
pilot le pilote
PIN le code
pin l'épingle (f)

pineapple l'ananas (m)
pink rose
pipe (for smoking) la
pipe; (for water) le
tuyau
piston le piston
pizza la pizza
place l'endroit (m); *at
your place* chez vous
planner l'agenda (m)
plant la plante
plaster le pansement
plastic le plastique
plastic bag le sac
plastique
plastic wrap le film
alimentaire
transparent
plate l'assiette (f)
platform le quai
play (theater) la pièce;
(verb) jouer
please s'il vous plaît
*pleased: pleased to meet
you* enchanté(e)
plug (electrical) la
prise; (sink) le
bouchon
plumber (occupation)
le plombier
pocket la poche
poison le poison
police la police
police officer le policier
police report le rapport
de police
police station le
commissariat
politics la politique
poor pauvre; (bad
quality) mauvais
pop music la musique
pop
pork le porc
port (harbor) le port;
(drink) le porto
porter le porteur
possible possible
postal (ZIP) *code* le
code postal
postcard la carte postale
poster (outside)
l'affiche (f); (inside)
le poster
post office la poste
potato la pomme de
terre
poultry la volaille
pound (weight) la livre
powder la poudre
prefer préférer
prepared meals les plats
préparés (m)
prescription
l'ordonnance (f)
pretty (beautiful) joli;
(quite) plutôt
price le prix
priest le prêtre
printer
l'imprimante (f)
private privé

problem le problème
profession la profession
professor le professeur
profits
les bénéfices (m)
public le public
pull tirer
puncture (tire) la
crevaison
purple violet
purse le porte-monnaie
push pousser
put mettre
pyjamas le pyjama

Q

quality la qualité
quarter le quart
question la question
quick rapide
quiet (preson)
silencieux; (street,
etc.) tranquille
quite (fairly) assez

R

rabbit le lapin
radiator le radiateur
radio la radio
radish le radis
rail: by rail par chemin
de fer
railroad le chemin de
fer
rain la pluie
raincoat
l'imperméable (m)
raisin le raisin sec
rake le râteau
rare (uncommon)
rare; (steak) saignant
rash la rougeur
raspberry la framboise
rat le rat
razor blades les lames
de rasoir (f)
read lire
reading lamp la lampe
de bureau; (bedside)
la lampe de chevet
ready prêt
receipt le reçu
reception la réception
receptionist le/la
receptionniste
record (music) le
disque; (sports, etc.)
le record
record player le tourne-
disque
record store le disquaire
red rouge; (hair) roux
refreshments les
rafraîchissements (m)
refrigerator le frigo
registered mail en
recommandé
relax se détendre
religion la religion

remember: I remember je m'en souviens; *I don't remember* je ne me souviens pas

rent (verb) louer

reservation la réservation

reserve (verb) réserver

rest (remainder) le reste; (verb: relax) se reposer

restaurant le restaurant

restaurant car le wagon-restaurant

restrooms les toilettes (f)

return (come back) revenir; (give back) rendre

rice le riz

rich riche

right (correct) juste; (not left) la droite

ring (jewelry) la bague

ripe mûr

river le fleuve

road la route; (in town) la rue

roasted rôti

rock (stone) le rocher; (music) le rock

roll (bread) le petit pain

roof le toit

room la chambre; (space) la place

room service le room service

rope la corde

rose la rose

round (circular) rond; *it's my round* c'est ma tournée (buying drinks)

round-trip ticket l'aller retour (m)

roundabout le rond-point

row (verb) ramer

rowboat la barque

rubber (material) le caoutchouc

rug (mat) la carpette; (blanket) la couverture

rugby le rugby

ruins les ruines (f)

ruler la règle

rum le rhum

run (verb) courir

runway la piste

S

sad triste

safe (not in danger) en sécurité; (not dangerous) sans danger

safety pin l'épingle de nourrice (f)

sailing la voile

sailboat le voilier

salad la salade

sale la vente; (at reduced prices) les soldes (f)

salmon le saumon

salt le sel

same: the same ... le/la même ...; *the same again, please* la même chose, s'il vous plaît

sand le sable

sandals les sandales (f)

sand dunes les dunes (f)

sandwich le sandwich

sanitary napkins les serviettes hygiéniques (f)

Saturday samedi

sauce la sauce

saucer la soucoupe

saucepan la casserole

sauna le sauna

sausage la saucisse

say dire; *what did you say?* qu'avez-vous dit?; *how do you say ...?* comment dit-on ...?

scarf l'écharpe (f); (head) le foulard

schedule l'emploi du temps (m); (train, bus) l'horaire (f)

school l'école (f)

science la science

scissors les ciseaux (m)

Scotland l'Ecosse (f)

screen l'écran (m)

screw la vis

screwdriver le tournevis

sea la mer

seafood les fruits de mer (m)

seat la place

seat belt la ceinture de sécurité

second (of time) la seconde; (in series) deuxième

second class en seconde

secretary le/la secrétaire

see voir; *I can't see* je ne vois rien; *I see* je vois

self-employed à mon compte

sell vendre

seminar le séminaire

send envoyer

separate (adj) séparé; (verb) séparer

September septembre

serious sérieux

seven sept

seventeen dix-sept

seventy soixante-dix

several plusieurs

sew coudre

shampoo le shampooing

shave: to shave se raser

shaving foam la mousse à raser

shawl le châle

she elle

sheet le drap

shell la coquille

shellfish les crustacés (m)

ship le bateau

shirt la chemise

shoelaces les lacets (m)

shoemaker la cordonnerie

shoe polish le cirage

shoes les chaussures (f)

shop le magasin

shopkeeper commerçant; (fem) commerçante

shopping les courses (f); *to go shopping* faire les courses

short court; petit

shorts le short

shoulder l'épaule (f)

shower (bath) la douche; (rain) l'averse (f)

shower gel le gel douche

shrimp la crevette

shutter (camera) l'obturateur (m); (window) le volet

sick: I feel sick j'ai envie de vomir; *to be sick* (vomit) vomir

side (edge) le bord

sidelights les feux de position (m)

sidewalk le trottoir

sightseeing le tourism

silk la soie

silver (color) argenté; (metal) l'argent (m)

simple simple

sing chanter

single (one) seul; (unmarried) célibataire

single room la chambre pour une personne; la chambre simple

sink l'évier (m)

sir monsieur

sister la sœur

six six

sixteen seize

sixty soixante

size la taille

skates les patins à glace (m)

ski le ski; (verb) skier

ski boots les chaussures de ski (f)

skid (verb) déraper

skiing: to go skiing faire du ski

ski lift le remonte-pente

skin cleanser le démaquillant
ski pole le bâton de ski
ski resort la station de ski
skirt la jupe
sky le ciel
sled la luge
sleep le sommeil; (verb) dormir
sleeper car le wagon-lit
sleeping bag le sac de couchage
sleeping pill le somnifère
sleeve la manche
slip le jupon
slippers les pantoufles (f)
slow lent
small petit
la rivière; (big)
smell l'odeur (f); (verb) sentir
smart intelligent
smile le sourire; (verb) sourire
smoke la fumée; (verb) fumer
snack le snack
snow la neige
so si
soaking solution (for contact lenses) la solution de trempage
soap le savon
soccer le football
socks les chaussettes (f)
soft mou
soft lenses les lentilles souples (f)
soil la terre
somebody quelqu'un
somehow d'une façon ou d'une autre
something quelque chose
sometimes quelquefois
somewhere quelque part
son le fils
song la chanson
sorry (apology) pardon; *sorry?* (pardon?) pardon?; *I'm sorry* je suis désolé
soup la soupe
south le sud
souvenir le souvenir
spade (shovel) la pelle; (garden) la bêche
spades (cards) pique
Spain l'Espagne (f)
Spanish espagnol
spare parts les pièces de rechange (f)
spark plug la bougie
sparkling water l'eau gazeuse (f)

speak parler; *do you speak ...?* parlez-vous ...?; *I don't speak ...* je ne parle pas ...
speed la vitesse
speed limit la limitation de vitesse
spider l'araignée (f)
spinach les épinards (m)
spoon la cuillère
sport le sport
spring (mechanical) le ressort; (season) le printemps
square (in town) la place; (adj: shape) carré
stadium le stade
staircase l'escalier (m)
stairs les escaliers (m)
stamp le timbre
stand in line faire la queue
stapler l'agrafeuse (f)
star l'étoile (f); (movie) la vedette
start (beginning) le début; (verb) commencer
statement la déposition
station la gare; (metro) la station
statue la statue
steak le steak
steal voler; *it's been stolen* on l'a volé
steamed à la vapeur
steamer le bateau à vapeur; (cooking) le couscoussier
steering wheel le volant
sting la piqûre; (verb) piquer
stockings les bas (m)
stomach l'estomac (m)
stomachache le mal de ventre, le mal à l'estomac
stop (bus) l'arrêt (de bus) (m); (verb) s'arrêter
storm la tempête
stove la cuisinière
straight ahead tout droit
strawberry la fraise
stream (small river) le ruisseau
street la rue
street musician le musicien des rues
string (cord) la ficelle; (guitar, etc.) la corde
stroller la poussette
strong (person, drink) fort; (material) résistant
student l'étudiant (m)
stupid stupide
suburbs la banlieue
subway le métro

sugar le sucre
suit le costume; *it suits you* ça vous va bien
suitcase la valise
summer l'été (m)
sun le soleil
sunbathe se faire bronzer
sunburn le coup de soleil
Sunday dimanche
sunglasses les lunettes de soleil (f)
sunny ensoleillé
sunshade le parasol
suntan le bronzage
suntan lotion la lotion solaire
supermarket le supermarché
supper le souper
supplement le supplément
suppository le suppositoire
sure sûr
suspenders (clothes) les bretelles (f)
sweat la transpiration; (verb) transpirer
sweater le pull, le gilet
sweatshirt le sweat-shirt
sweet (not sour) sucré
swim (verb) nager
swimming la natation; *to go swimming* aller se baigner
swimming pool la piscine
swimming trunks le maillot de bain
swimsuit le maillot de bain
Swiss suisse(sse)
switch l'interrupteur (m)
Switzerland la Suisse
synagogue la synagogue
syringe la seringue
syrup le sirop

T

table la table
tablet le cachet
take prendre
to go (food) à emporter
takeoff le décollage
talcum powder le talc
talk la conversation; (verb) parler
tall grand
tampon le tampon
tangerine la mandarine
tap (water) le robinet
tapestry la tapisserie
taxi le taxi
tea le thé
teacher (secondary) le professeur

telephone le téléphone; (verb) téléphoner

telephone box la cabine téléphonique

television la télévision

teller le guichet

temperature la température

ten dix

tennis le tennis

tennis shoes les tennis (m)

tent la tente

tent peg le piquet de tente

tent pole le montant de tente

terminal le terminal

terrace la terrasse

than que

thank (verb) remercier; thank you merci; thanks merci

that (that one) ça; that bus ce bus; that man cet homme; that woman cette femme; what's that? qu'est-ce que c'est?; I think that the ... je pense que le ...

the le/la; (plural) les

theater le théâtre

their: their room leur chambre; their books leurs livres; it's theirs c'est à eux

them: it's them ce sont eux/elles; it's for them c'est pour eux/elles; give it to them donnez-le-leur

then alors; (after) ensuite

there là; there is/are ... il y a ...

these: these things ces choses; these are mine ils sont à moi

they ils; (fem) elles

thick épais

thief le voleur

thin mince, maigre

think penser; I think so je pense que oui; I'll think about it je vais y penser

third troisième

thirsty: I'm thirsty j'ai soif

thirteen treize

thirty trente

this (this one) ceci; this bus ce bus; this man cet homme; this woman cette femme; what's this? qu'est-ce que c'est?; this is Mr ... je vous présente M. ...

those: those things ces choses-là; those are his ils sont à lui

three trois

throat la gorge

throat lozenges les pastilles pour la gorge (f)

through à travers

thumbtack la punaise

thunderstorm l'orage (m)

Thursday jeudi

ticket le billet; (metro, bus) le ticket

ticket collector le contrôleur

ticket office le guichet

tide la marée

tie la cravate; (verb) nouer

tight étroit

tiles, tiling le carrelage

time l'heure (f); what's the time? quelle heure est-il?

tip (money) le pourboire; (end) le bout

tire le pneu

tired fatigué

tissues mouchoirs

to: to America en Amérique; to Paris à Paris; to the station à la gare; to the center au centre; to the doctor chez le docteur

toast le pain grillé

tobacco le tabac

toboggan le toboggan

today aujourd'hui

together ensemble

toilet paper le papier hygiénique

tomato la tomate

tomorrow demain; see you tomorrow à demain

tongue la langue

tonic le tonic

tonight ce soir

too (also) aussi; (excessively) trop

tooth la dent

toothache le mal de dents

toothbrush la brosse à dents

toothpaste le dentifrice

tour la visite

tourist le/la touriste

tourist office le syndicat d'initiative

towel la serviette

tower la tour

town la ville

town hall l'hôtel de ville (m); la mairie

toy le jouet

tractor le tracteur

trade fair la foire-exposition

tradition la tradition

traffic la circulation, le trafic

traffic lights les feux (m)

trailer la remorque

train le train

trainee le stagiaire

translate traduire

translator le traducteur

trash bag le sac poubelle

trash can la poubelle

travel agency l'agence de voyages (f)

traveler's check le chèque de voyage

tray le plateau

tree l'arbre (m)

truck le camion

true vrai

trunk (car) le coffre

try essayer

Tuesday mardi

tunnel le tunnel

turn signal le clignotant

tweezers la pince à épiler

twelve douze

twenty vingt

two deux

U

ugly laid

umbrella le parapluie

uncle l'oncle (m)

under ... sous ...

underpants le slip

understand comprendre; I understand je comprends; I don't understand je ne comprends pas

underwear les sous-vêtements (f)

university l'université (f)

unleaded sans plomb

until jusqu'à

unusual inhabituel

up en haut; (upward) vers le haut; up there là-haut

urgent urgent

us: it's us c'est nous; it's for us c'est pour nous; give it to us donnez-le-nous

use (verb) utiliser; it's no use ça ne sert à rien

useful utile

usual habituel

usually d'habitude

V

vacancy (room) la chambre à louer
vacation les vacances (f)
vaccination la vaccination
vacuum cleaner l'aspirateur (m)
valley la vallée
valve la soupape
vanilla la vanille
vase le vase
VCR le magnètoscope
veal le veau
vegetables les légumes (m)
vegetarian (adj) végétarien
vehicle le véhicule
very très; very much beaucoup
veterinarian le vétérinaire
video (film/tape) la vidéo
view la vue
viewfinder le viseur
villa la villa
village le village
vinegar le vinaigre
violin le violon
visit la visite; (verb: place) visiter; (person) rendre visite
visitor le visiteur
vitamin pill le comprimé de vitamines
vodka la vodka
voice la voix
voicemail la messagerie téléphonique

W

wait attendre; wait! attendez!
waiter le serveur; waiter! garçon!
waiting room la salle d'attente
waitress la serveuse; waitress! Mademoiselle!
Wales le pays de Galles
walk (verb) marcher; to go for a walk aller se promener
wall (inside) la paroi; (outside) le mur
wallet le portefeuille
want (verb) vouloir; I would like je voudrais
war la guerre
wardrobe l'armoire (f)
warm chaud
was: I was j'étais; he was il était; she was elle était; it was il/elle était
washer la rondelle

washing machine la machine à laver
wasp la guêpe
watch la montre; (verb) regarder
water l'eau (f)
waterfall la chute d'eau
water heater le chauffe-eau
wave la vague; (verb) faire signe de la main
wavy (hair) ondulé
we nous
weather le temps
Website le site web
wedding le mariage
Wednesday mercredi
weeds les mauvais herbes (f)
week la semaine
welcome: you're welcome je vous en prie
Wellington boots les boîtes en caoutchouc (f)
were: we were nous étions; you were vous étiez; they were ils/elles étaient
west l'ouest
wet mouillé
what? comment?; what is it? qu'est-ce que c'est?
wheel la roue
wheelchair le fauteuil roulant; la chaise roulante
when? quand?
where? où?
whether si
which? lequel?
whiskey le whisky
white blanc, (fem) blanche
who? qui?
why? pourquoi?
wide large
wife la femme
wind le vent
window la fenêtre
windshield le pare-brise
wine le vin
wine list la carte des vins
wine merchant le négociant en vins
wing l'aile (f)
winter l'hiver (m)
with avec; with pleasure avec plasir
withdraw (verb) retirer
without sans
witness le témoin
woman la femme
wood le bois
wool la laine
word le mot

work le travail; (verb) travailler; (machine, etc.) fonctionner
worse pire
worst le pire
wrapping paper le papier d'emballage; (for presents) le papier cadeau
wrench la clé anglaise
wrist le poignet
write (verb) écrire; written by écrit par
writing paper le papier à lettres
wrong faux, (fem) fausse

X, Y, Z

X-ray radio
X-ray departement la salle de radiologie
year l'an (m); l'année (f)
yellow jaune
yes oui
yesterday hier
yet déjà; not yet pas encore
yogurt le yaourt
you (singular informal) tu; (plural; singular formal) vous
young jeune
your (singular informal): your book ton livre; your house ta maison; your shoes tes chaussures; it's yours c'est à toi (plural; singular formal): your house votre maison; your shoes vos chaussures; it's yours c'est à vous
youth hostel l'auberge de jeunesse (f)
zipper la fermeture éclair
zoo le zoo
zucchini la courgette

Dictionary
French *to* English

The gender of French nouns listed here is indicated by the abbreviations "(m)" and "(f)," for masculine and feminine. Plural nouns are indicated by "(m pl)" or "(f pl)." French adjectives (adj) vary according to the gender and number of the word they describe; the masculine form is shown here. In most cases, you add an **-e** to the masculine form to make it feminine. Certain endings use a different rule: masculine adjectives that end in **-x** adopt an **-se** ending in the feminine form, while those that end in **-ien** change to **-ienne**. Some feminine adjectives that do not follow these rules are shown here and follow the abbreviation "(fem)." For the plural form, a (silent) **-s** is usually added.

A

à: *at:* à la poste *at the post office;* à trois heures *at 3 o'clock;* à côté de *beside;* à demain *see you tomorrow;* à emporter *to go* (food); à travers *through*

abat-jour (m) *lampshade*

abricot (m) *apricot*

accélérateur (m) *accelerator*

accident (m) *accident*

acheter *to buy*

adaptateur (m) *adapter* (voltage)

addition (f) *check* (in restaurant)

adhésif (m) *adhesive*

adresse (f) *address*

adresse électronique (f) *email address*

aéroglisseur (m) *hovercraft*

aéroport (m) *airport*

affaire (f) *bargain*

affaires (f pl) *business*

affiche (f) *poster* (outside)

affreux *awful*

agence de voyages (f) *travel agency*

agenda (m) *planner*

agent (m) *agent*

agneau (m) *lamb*

agrafeuse (f) *stapler*

agrandissement (m) *enlargement*

aide (f) *help*

aider *to help*

aiguille (f) *needle;* aiguille à tricoter *knitting needle*

ail (m) *garlic*

aile (f) *wing*

ailleurs *somewhere else*

aimer *to like/love;* j'aime nager *I like swimming;* je n'aime pas *I don't like*

air (m) *air*

alcool (m) *alcohol*

Algérie (f) *Algeria*

algérien(ne) *Algerian*

allée (f) *path*

Allemagne (f) *Germany*

allemand(e) *German*

aller *to go*

aller chercher *to get* (fetch)

allergique *allergic*

aller patiner *to go ice-skating*

aller retour (m) *round-trip ticket*

aller simple (m) *one-way ticket*

allez-vous en! *go away!*

allumage (m) *ignition*

allumette (f) *match* (light)

alors *well then*

Alpes: les Alpes (m pl) *Alps*

amant (m) *lover*

ambassade (f) *embassy*

ambulance (f) *ambulance*

amer *bitter*

américain(e) *American*

Amérique (f) *America*

ami(e) *friend*

amical *friendly*

amour (m) *love*

amphithéâtre (m) *lecture hall*

ampoule (f) *blister; light bulb*

an (m) *year*

ananas (m) *pineapple*

Andorre *Andorra*

anglais(e) *English*

Angleterre (f) *England*

animaux (familiers) (m pl) *pets*

animé *busy* (street)

année (f) *year*

anniversaire (m) *birthday*

annuaire (m) *directory* (telephone)

antigel (m) *antifreeze*

antiseptique (m) *antiseptic*

août *August*

apéritif (m) *aperitif*

appareil acoustique (m) *hearing aid*

appareil-photo (m) *camera*

appartement (m) *apartment*

appât (m) *bait*

appétit (m) *appetite*

apprendre *to learn*

après *after*

après-midi (m) *afternoon*

après-rasage (m) *aftershave*

araignée (f) *spider*

arbre (m) *tree*

arbre à cames (m) *camshaft*

architecture (f) *architecture*

arête (f) *fish bone*

argent (m) *cash; money; silver* (metal)

argenté *silver* (color)

armoire (f) *wardrobe*

arrêt de bus (m) *bus stop*

arrière (m) *back* (not front)

arrivée (f) *arrival*
arriver *to arrive*
art (m) *art*
artiste (m) *artist*
ascenseur (m) *elevator*
aspirateur (m) *vacuum cleaner*
aspirine (f) *aspirin*
assez *enough; fairly*
assiette (f) *plate*
assurance (f) *insurance*
asthmatique *asthmatic*
attaché-case (m) *briefcase*
attendez! *wait!*
attendre *to wait*
attention! *careful!*
atterrir *to land*
attirant *attractive*
au: au café *at the café;* au revoir *goodbye*
auberge (f) *inn*
auberge de jeunesse (f) *youth hostel*
aucun *not any; none*
au-dessus de *over (above)*
aujourd'hui *today*
aussi *too (also)*
Australie (f) *Australia*
australien(ne) *Australian*
automatique *automatic*
automne (m) *autumn*
autoroute (f) *highway, freeway*
autre: autre chose *something else*
avance (f) *advance*
avant *before*
avec *with;* avec plasir *I'd love to*
averse (f) *shower (rain)*
aveugle *blind (cannot see)*
avion (m) *aircraft*
avocat (m) *avocado*
avocat(e) *lawyer*
avoir *to have*
avril *April*

B

bac (m) *ferry (small)*
bagages (m pl) *luggage; baggage;* bagages à main (m pl) *carry-on luggage*
baigner: aller se baigner *to go swimming*
bain (m) *bath*
balai (m) *broom*
balcon (m) *balcony*
balle (f) *ball (tennis, etc.)*

ballon (m) *ball (soccer, etc.)*
banane (f) *banana*
bandage (m) *bandage*
banlieue (f) *suburbs*
banque (f) *bank*
bar (m) *bar (place)*
barbe (f) *beard*
barbecue (m) *barbecue*
barque (f) *rowboat*
bas (m) *stockings; low (adj);* en bas *down*
bateau (m) *boat; ship;* bateau à moteur (m) *motorboat;* bateau à vapeur (m) *steamer*
bâtiment (m) *building*
bâton de ski (m) *ski pole*
batterie (f) *battery (car)*
baume après-shampooing (m) *conditioner (hair)*
beau, (fem) belle *beautiful*
bébé (m) *baby*
bêche (f) *spade (garden)*
beige *beige*
beignet (m) *doughnut*
belge *Belgian*
Belgique: la Belgique *Belgium*
bénéfices (m pl) *profits*
béquilles (f pl) *crutches*
besoin: avoir besoin de *to need;* j'ai besoin de ... *I need ...*
beurre (m) *butter*
bibliothèque (f) *library*
bicyclette (f) *bicycle*
bien sûr *of course*
bien! *good!;* ça vous va bien *it suits you*
bière (f) *beer*
bijouterie (f) *jeweler*
billet (m) *ticket; bank note*
biscuit (m) *cookie*
blanc, (fem) blanche *white*
blanchisserie (f) *laundry (place)*
blême *pale*
blessure (f) *injury*
bleu (m) *bruise;* bleu *blue (adj)*
bloc notes (m) *notepad*
blond (adj) *blond*
bœuf (m) *beef*
boire *to drink;* vous voulez boire quelque chose? *would you like something to drink?*
bois (m) *wood*
boisson (f) *drink*
boîte (f) *box;* boîte à lettres *mailbox;* boîte de chocolats *box of chocolates;* boîte de

conserve *can (vessel);* boîte de nuit *nightclub;* boîte de vitesses *gearbox*
boîtes en caoutchouc (f pl) *Wellington boots*
bol (m) *bowl*
bon, (fem) bonne *good*
bonbon (m) *sweet (confectionery);* bonbons à la menthe (m pl) *peppermints*
bondé *crowded*
bonjour *hello*
bon marché *inexpensive; cheap*
bonne chance! *good luck!*
bonsoir *good evening*
bord (m) *side (edge)*
botte (f) *boot (footwear)*
bouche (f) *mouth*
boucherie (f) *butcher shop*
bouchon (m) *plug (sink); cork*
boucles (f pl) *curls*
boucles d'oreille (f pl) *earrings*
bouger *to move;* ne bougez pas! *don't move!*
bougie (f) *spark plug; candle*
bouilli *boiled*
bouillir *to boil*
bouilloire (f) *kettle*
boulangerie (f) *bread shop*
bout (m) *tip, end*
bouteille (f) *bottle*
bouton (m) *button;* boutons de manchette (m pl) *cufflinks*
bracelet (m) *bracelet*
branche (f) *branch*
bras (m) *arm*
Bretagne: la Bretagne *Brittany*
bretelles (f pl) *suspenders (clothes)*
briquet (m) *lighter*
britannique *British*
broche (f) *brooch*
brochure (f) *brochure*
broderie (f) *embroidery*
bronzage (m) *suntan*
bronzer: se faire bronzer *to sunbathe*
brosse (f) *brush;* brosse à dents (f) *toothbrush*
brosser *to brush*
brouillard (m) *fog*
brûler *to burn*
brûlure (f) *burn*
Bruxelles *Brussels*
bruyant *noisy*
budget (m) *budget*
bunker (m) *bunker*

bureau (m) *desk; office*
bureau de location (m)
 box office
bus (m) *bus*

C

ça *that* (that one)
cabine téléphonique (f)
 telephone booth
cacahuètes (f pl)
 peanuts
cachet (m) *tablet*
cadeau (m) *gift*
cadenas (m) *padlock*
cadre (m) *executive*
 (in company)
cafard (m) *cockroach*
café (m) *café; coffee;*
 café crème *coffee with*
 milk; café soluble
 instant coffee
cage (f) *cage*
caisse (f) *checkout*
 (supermarket)
calculette (f)
 calculator
cambriolage (m)
 burglary
caméscope (m)
 camcorder
camion (m) *truck*
campagne (f)
 countryside
camping-car (m)
 camper van
Canada (m) *Canada*
canadien(ne)
 Canadian
canal (m) *canal*
canif (m) *penknife*
canne à pêche (f)
 fishing rod
canoë (m) *canoe*
caoutchouc (m)
 rubber (material)
capot (m) *car hood*
capsule (f) *cap* (bottle)
caravane (f) *camper*
 trailer
carburateur (m)
 carburetor
carnet (m) *notebook;*
 carnet de chèques
 (m) *checkbook*
carotte (f) *carrot*
carpette (f) *rug* (mat)
carré *square* (adj:
 shape)
carreau *diamonds*
 (cards)
carrelage (m) *tiles,*
 tiling
carte (f) *menu; card;*
 map; carte bancaire
 debit card; carte de
 crédit *credit card;*
 carte d'embarquement
 boarding pass; carte
 des vins *wine list;*
 carte de visite *business*

card; carte postale
postcard; carte
téléphonique *phone*
card
casquette (f) *cap* (hat)
cassé *broken*
casserole (f) *saucepan*
cassette (f) *cassette*
cassis (m)
 black currant
cathédrale (f)
 cathedral
cave (f) *cellar*
ce (bus) *that (bus)*
ceci *this* (this one)
ceinture (f) *belt;*
 ceinture de sécurité
 seat belt
célibataire *single*
 (unmarried)
cellule photoélectrique
 (f) *light meter*
cendrier (m) *ashtray*
cent *hundred*
centre (m) *center;*
 centre sportif (m)
 sports center
centre-ville (m) *down-*
 town, town center
cerise (f) *cherry*
certificat (m)
 certificate
ces (choses) *these*
 (things)
c'est *it's;* c'est tout
 that's all
cet (homme) *that (man)*
cette (femme) *that*
 (woman)
chaise (f) *chair*
châle (m) *shawl*
chambre (f) *bedroom;*
 chambre à louer
 vacancy; chambre
 pour deux personnes
 double room; chambre
 simple *single room*
chambre à air (f) *inner*
 tube
champ (m) *field*
 (farming)
champignon (m)
 mushroom
chance (f) *luck*
changer *to change*
 (money); se changer
 to change (clothes)
chanson (f) *song*
chanter *to sing*
chapeau (m) *hat*
chaque *each; every*
charcuterie (f)
 delicatessen
chargeur (m) *charger*
chariot (m) *cart*
charpentier (m)
 carpenter
chat (m) *cat*
château (m) *castle*
chaud *hot; warm;*
 j'ai chaud *I feel hot*

chauffage (m) *heating;*
 chauffage central
 central heating
chauffe-eau (m) *boiler;*
 water heater
chaussettes (f pl) *socks*
chaussures (f pl) *shoes;*
 chaussures de ski
 (f pl) *ski boots*
chauve *bald*
chef (m) *manager; chef*
 d'orchestre *conductor*
 (orchestra); chef de
 train *conductor* (train)
chemin (m) *path*
chemin de fer (m)
 railroad
cheminée (f) *fireplace;*
 chimney
chemise (f) *shirt;*
 chemise de nuit
 nightgown
chemisier (m) *blouse*
chèque (m) *check;*
 chèque de voyage
 traveler's check
cher *expensive;* pas
 cher *inexpensive*
cheveux (m pl) *hair;*
 les cheveux
 longs/courts
 long/short hair
cheville (f) *ankle*
chez *at home;* chez moi;
 at my house; chez
 vous *at your place*
chien (m) *dog*
chiffon à poussière (m)
 duster
chiffres (m pl) *figures*
chips (f pl) *chips*
chocolat (m) *chocolate*
chou (m) *cabbage*
chou-fleur (m)
 cauliflower
chute d'eau (f)
 waterfall
ciel (m) *sky*
cigare (m) *cigar*
cigarette (f) *cigarette*
cimetière (m)
 cemetery
cinéma (m) *movie*
 theater, cinema
cinq *five*
cinquante *fifty*
cintre (m) *coathanger*
cirage (m) *shoe polish*
circulation (f) *traffic*
ciseaux (m pl)
 scissors
citron (m) *lemon;* citron
 vert *lime*
clair *clear; light* (not
 dark)
classe (f) *class*
clavier (m) *keyboard*
clé (f) *key;* clé anglaise
 (f) *wrench*
clignotant (m)
 turn signal

climatisation (f) *air conditioning*
cloche (f) *bell* (church)
clou (m) *nail* (metal)
cocktail (m) *cocktail party*
code (m) *PIN*
code de la route (m) *highway code*
code postal (m) *postal (ZIP) code*
cœur (m) *heart;* problème au cœur *heart condition;* cœurs (m pl) *hearts* (cards)
coffre (m) *trunk* (car)
cognac (m) *brandy*
coiffeur (m) *hairdresser; barber's*
coin (m) *corner*
col (m) *collar*
colis (m) *parcel*
collants (m pl) *pantyhose*
colle (f) *glue*
collection (f) *collection* (stamps, etc.)
collier (m) *collar; necklace*
colline (f) *hill*
combien? *how much?;* combien ça coûte? *how much does it cost?*
comme *like* (similar to)
commencer *to start*
comment? *how?;* comment allez-vous? *how are you?;* comment est-ce que ça s'appelle? *what's it called?;* comment vous appelez-vous? *what's your name?*
commerçant(e) *shopkeeper*
commissariat (m) *police station*
commode (f) *dresser*
compagnie (f) *company;* compagnie aérienne *airline*
compartiment (m) *compartment*
complet *full*
compliqué *complicated*
comprendre *to understand;* je comprends *I understand;* je ne comprends pas *I don't understand*
comprimé (m) *pill;* comprimé de vitamines *vitamin pill*
comptable (m/f) *accountant*

compte: à mon compte *self-employed*
concert (m) *concert*
concierge (m/f) *caretaker*
concombre (m) *cucumber*
conducteur (m) *driver*
conduire *to drive*
conférence (f) *conference*
confiseur (m) *candy store*
confiture (f) *jam*
congélateur (m) *freezer*
connaître *to know* (person)
consigne automatique (f) *luggage lockers*
constructeur (m) *builder*
consulat (m) *consulate*
consultant(e) *consultant*
contraceptif (m) *contraceptive*
contre *against*
contrôle des passeports (m) *passport control*
contrôleur (m) *ticket collector*
conversation (f) *talk*
copieur (m) *photocopier*
coquille (f) *shell*
corde (f) *rope; string* (guitar, etc.)
cordonnerie (f) *shoemaker*
corne (f) *horn* (animal)
corps (m) *body*
correspondant (m) *pen pal*
corse *Corsican*
Corse: la Corse *Corsica*
costume (m) *suit*
côtelette (f) *chop* (food)
coton (m) *cotton;* coton hydrophile *cotton balls*
cou (m) *neck*
couche (f) *diaper;* couches à jeter (f pl) *disposable diapers*
coude (m) *elbow*
coudre *to sew*
couette (f) *comforter* (bedding)
couleur (f) *color*
couloir (m) *corridor*
coup de soleil (m) *sunburn*
coupe (de cheveux) (f) *haircut*
couper *to cut, chop*
coupure (f) *cut*

courant (m) *current*
courgette (f) *zucchini*
courir *to run*
courroie du ventilateur (f) *fan belt*
courses (f pl) *shopping; to go shopping* faire les courses
court *short*
couscoussier (m) *steamer* (cooking)
cousin (m) *cousin*
couteau (m) *knife*
coûter *to cost*
couverture (f) *blanket; rug*
crabe (m) *crab*
crampe (f) *cramp*
cravate (f) *tie*
crayon (m) *pencil*
crème (f) *cream;* crème anti-insecte (f) *insect repellent cream*
crêpe (f) *crêpe*
crevaison (f) *puncture* (tire)
crevette (f) *shrimp*
crier *to cry* (shout)
croisière (f) *cruise*
crustacés (m) *shellfish*
cuillère (f) *spoon*
cuir (m) *leather*
cuire *to bake*
cuisine (f) *kitchen*
cuisinier (m) *cook*
cuisinière (f) *stove*
curry (m) *curry*

D

d'accord *OK*
danger (m) *danger;* sans danger *safe*
dans *in*
danse (f) *dance*
danser *to dance*
de *of*
début (m) *start* (beginning)
débutant(e) *beginner*
décapsuleur (m) *bottle opener*
décembre *December*
décollage (m) *takeoff*
décolorer *to bleach*
décorateur (m) *decorator*
dehors *outside*
déjà *yet; already*
déjeuner (m) *lunch*
delco (m) *distributor* (car)
demain *tomorrow*
démaquillant (m) *skin cleanser*
déménager *to move* (change homes)
demi *half;* une demi-heure *half an hour*

demi-pension (f) *half-board*

dent (f) *tooth*

dentelle (f) *lace*

dentier (m) *dentures*

dentifrice (m) *toothpaste*

dentiste (m/f) *dentist*

déodorant (m) *deodorant*

départ (m) *departures*

département (f) *department*

dépliant (m) *leaflet*

déposition (f) *statement*

déraper *skid* (verb)

dernier *last* (final); la semaine dernière *last week*

derrière *behind*

descendre *to get off* (bus, etc.)

designer (m) *designer*

désolé: je suis désolé(e) *I'm sorry*

desserts (m pl) *desserts*

détritus (m) *garbage*

deux *two*; les deux *both*

deuxième *second* (in series)

devant *in front of*

développer *to develop*

d'habitude *usually*

diabétique *diabetic*

diamant (m) *diamond* (jewel)

diarrhée (f) *diarrhea*

dictionnaire (m) *dictionary*

diesel (m) *diesel*

différent *different*; c'est différent *that's different*

difficile *difficult*

dimanche *Sunday*

dîner (m) *dinner*

dire *to say*; qu'avez-vous dit? *what did you say?*; comment dit-on ...? *how do you say ...?*; qu'est-ce que cela veut dire? *what does this mean?*

directeur (m) *director*

discothèque (m) *disco*

disquaire (m) *record store*

disque (m) *record* (music); disque compact (m) *CD* (compact disc)

distributeur automatique (m) *ATM*

divertissement (m) *entertainment*

divorcé *divorced*

dix *ten*

dix-huit *eighteen*

dix-neuf *nineteen*

dix-sept *seventeen*

docteur (m) *doctor*

document (m) *document*

doigt (m) *finger*

dois: je dois ... *I must ...*

dollar (m) *dollar*

donner *give*

dormir *to sleep*

dos (m) *back* (body)

douane (f) *customs*

doubler *to overtake* (in a car)

douche (f) *shower* (bath)

douleur (f) *ache; pain*

douze *twelve*

drap (m) *sheet*

drapeau (m) *flag*

draps (m pl) *bed linen*

droit (m) *law*

droite *right* (not left)

drôle *funny*

dunes (f pl) *sand dunes*

dur *hard*

E

eau (f) *water*; eau gazeuse *sparkling water*; eau minérale *mineral water*; eau potable *drinking water*; eau de Javel *bleach*

échanger *to exchange*

écharpe (f) *scarf*

échecs (m pl) *chess*

école (f) *school*

Ecosse: l'Ecosse (f) *Scotland*

écouteurs (m) *headphones*

écran (m) *screen*

écrevisse (f) *crayfish* (freshwater)

écrire *to write*; écrit par ... *written by ...*

écrou (m) *nut* (for bolt)

église (f) *church*

élastique (m) *elastic band; elastic* (adj)

électricien(ne) *electrician*

électricité (f) *electricity*

électrique *electric*

elle *she*

elles *they* (fem)

email (m) *email*

embrayage (m) *clutch*

émeraude (f) *emerald*

emplacement (m) *pitch*

emploi du temps (m) *schedule*

en *in*; en France *in France*

enchanté(e) *pleased to meet you*

encore: encore un café *another cup of coffee*

encre (f) *ink*

endormi *asleep*

endroit (m) *place*

enfant (m) *child*

enfin! *at last!*

ennuyeux *boring*

enregistrement (m) *check-in*; enregistrement des bagages *baggage check-in*

ensemble *together*

ensoleillé *sunny*

ensuite *then* (after)

entendre *hear*

entre ... *between ...*

entrée (f) *entrance*

entrées (f pl) *starters*

enveloppe (f) *envelope*

envie: j'ai envie de ... *I feel like ...*

environ *about*

envoyer *to send*

épais *thick*

épaule (f) *shoulder*

épicerie (f) *grocery store*

épileptique *epileptic*

épinards (m) *spinach*

épingle (f) *pin*; épingle de nourrice *safety pin*

erreur (f) *mistake*

escalier (m) *stairs; staircase*; escalier roulant *escalator*

Espagne: l'Espagne (f) *Spain*

espagnol *Spanish*

essayer *to try*

essence (f) *gasoline*

essieu (m) *axle*

est (m) *east*

est *is*; il/elle est *he/she is*; c'est *it is*

estimation (f) *estimate*

estomac (m) *stomach*

et *and*

étage (m) *floor* (story)

été (m) *summer*

étiquette (f) *label*

étoile (f) *star*

étouffant *stuffy*

étranger (m) *foreigner*

étroit *narrow; tight*

étudiant (m) *student*

eux: c'est à eux *it's theirs*; c'est pour eux/elles *it's for them*

evanouir *to faint*

évier (m) *sink*

excédent de bagages (m) *excess baggage*

excellent *excellent*

excursion (f) *excursion*

exemple (m) *example*

exposition (f) *exhibition*

exprès *deliberately*

extérieure (m) *exterior*; *exterior* (adj) *exterior* extincteur (m) *fire extinguisher*

F

face: en face de *opposite*

facile *easy*

façon: d'une façon ou d'une autre *somehow*

facteur (m) *mail carrier*

facture (f) *invoice*

faim: j'ai faim *I'm hungry*

faire *to do; make*; faire de autostop *to hitchhike*; faire du jogging *to jog*; faire enregistrer ses bagages *to check in*; faire la cuisine *to cook*; faire la queue *to stand in line* (verb); faire signe de la main *to wave*

fan (m/f) *fan (enthusiast)*

fantastique *fantastic*

farine (f) *flour*

fatigué *tired*

fauteuil (m) *armchair*; fauteuil roulant (m) *wheelchair*

faux, (fem) fausse *wrong*

fax (m) *fax, fax machine*

félicitations! *congratulations!*

femme (f) *woman; wife*; femme de chambre *maid*; femme de ménages *cleaner*

fenêtre (f) *window*

fer à repasser (m) *iron (for clothes)*

ferme (f) *farm*

fermé *closed*

fermer *to close*

fermeture éclair (f) *zipper*

fermier (m) *farmer*

ferry (m) *ferry (large)*

fête (f) *party (celebration)*

feu (m) *fire*; feu d'artifice *fireworks*; feu de camp *campfire*

feuille (f) *leaf*

feutre (m) *felt-tip pen*

feux (m pl) *lights*; *traffic lights*; feux de position (m pl) *sidelights*

fevrier *February*

fiancé *engaged (couple)*

fiancé(e) *fiancé(e)*

ficelle (f) *string (cord)*

fièvre (f) *fever*

figue (f) *fig*

fille (f) *girl; daughter*

film (m) *film*

fils (m) *son*

fin (f) *end*

fini *over (finished)*

flash (m) *flash (camera)*

fleur (f) *flower*

fleuriste (f) *florist*

fleuve (m) *river (big)*

flûte (f) *flute*

foie (m) *liver*

foire (f) *fair*; foire-exposition *trade fair*

foncé *dark*; bleu foncé *dark blue*

fonctionner *function (machine, etc.)*

fond (m) *bottom*

football (m) *soccer*

forêt (f) *forest*

formulaire de demande (m) *application form*

fort *loud; strong (person, drink)*

fou, (fem) folle *mad*

foulard (m) *headscarf*

four (m) *oven*

fourchette (f) *fork*

frais, (fem) fraîche *cool*

fraise (f) *strawberry*

framboise (f) *raspberry*

français(e) *French*

France: la France *France*

frange (f) *fringe*

frein (m) *brake*; frein à main *handbrake*

freiner *to brake*

frère (m) *brother*

frigo (m) *refrigerator*

frire *to fry*

frit *fried*

frites (f pl) *chips*

froid (adj) *cold*

fromage (m) *cheese*

fromagerie (f) *cheese shop*

frontière (f) *border*

fruit (m) *fruit*

fruits de mer (m pl) *seafood*

fumée (f) *smoke*

fumer *to smoke*

fusil (m) *rifle*

G

galerie d'art (f) *art gallery*

gamelle (f) *animal's bowl*

gants (m pl) *gloves*

garage (m) *garage*

garagiste (m) *mechanic*

garantie (f) *guarantee*

garantir *to guarantee*

garçon (m) *boy*; garçon! *waiter!*

gare (f) *station*; gare routière (f) *bus station*

garer *to park*

garniture (f) *filling (in sandwich, cake)*

gâteau (m) *cake*

gauche *left (not right)*

gaz (m) *gas*; gaz à briquet (m) *lighter fluid*

gazoile (m) *diesel*

gel (m) *gel; frost*; gel douche (m) *shower gel*

gênant *embarrassing*

genou (m) *knee*

gens (m pl) *people*

gentil *friendly; kind*

gilet (m) *sweater*

gin (m) *gin*

gingembre (m) *ginger*

glace (f) *ice; ice cream*

golf (m) *golf*

gomme (f) *eraser*

gorge (f) *throat*

goût (m) *flavor*

goutes (f pl) *drops*

gouttière (f) *gutter*

gouvernement (m) *government*

grand *big; large; tall*; grand magasin (m) *department store*

Grande-Bretagne (f) *Great Britain*

grand-mère (f) *grandmother*

grand-père (m) *grandfather*

grands-parents (m pl) *grandparents*

gras (m) *fat (on meat, etc.)*

gratuit *free (of charge)*

grenier (m) *attic*

gril (m) *grill*

grillé(e) *grilled*

gris *gray*

gros, (fem) grosse (adj) *fat*

grotte (f) *cave*

groupe (m) *group; band (musicians)*

guêpe (f) *wasp*

guerre (f) *war*

gueule de bois (f) *hangover*

guichet (m) *cashier, teller; ticket office*

guide (m) *guide; guide book*; guide de conversation (m) *phrase book*

guitare (f) *guitar*

H

habituel *ordinary; usual*
hache (f) *ax*
haie (f) *hedge*
hamburger (m) *hamburger*
hamster (m) *hamster*
handicapé *disabled*
haricots (m pl) *beans*
haut *high;* en haut *up;* vers la haut *upward;* là-haut *up there*
hébergement (m) *accommodation*
hépatite (f) *hepatitis*
herbe (f) *grass*
heure (f) *hour; time*
heures d'ouverture (f pl) *opening times*
heureux *glad; happy*
hier *yesterday*
histoire (f) *history*
hiver (m) *winter*
homard (m) *lobster*
homéopathie *homeopathy*
homme (m) *man*
homosexuel *gay*
honnête *honest*
hôpital (m) *hospital*
horaire (f) *schedule* (train, bus)
horloge (f) *clock*
horrible *horrible*
hors-taxe *duty-free*
hôte (m) *host*
hôtel (m) *hotel*
hôtel de ville (m) *town hall*
hôtesse (f) *hostess;* hôtesse de air *flight attendant*
hoverport (m) *hoverport*
huile (f) *oil*
huit *eight*
huître (f) *oyster*
hydrofoil (m) *hydrofoil*

I

identification (f) *identification*
il *he; it* (m)
île (f) *island;* les îles Anglo-Normandes *Channel Islands*
ils *they* (m); ils sont *they are*
il y a ... *there is/are ...*
immédiatement *immediately*
imperméable (m) *raincoat*
impossible *impossible*
imprimante (f) *printer*
incendie (m) *fire* (blaze)

indigestion (f) *indigestion*
infection (f) *infection*
infirmier, (fem) infirmière *nurse*
information (f) *information*
informations (f pl) *news* (TV)
ingénierie (f) *engineering*
ingénieur (m) *engineer*
inhabituel *unusual*
insecte (m) *insect*
insomnie (f) *insomnia*
instrument de musique (m) *musical instrument*
intelligent *clever*
intéressant *interesting*
internet (m) *Internet*
interprète (m) *interpreter*
interpréter *to interpret*
interrupteur (m) *switch*
intoxication alimentaire (f) *food poisoning*
invitation (f) *invitation*
invité(e) *guest*
irlandais(e) *Irish*
Irlande (f) *Ireland*
Italie (f) *Italy*
italien(ne) *Italian*
ivre *drunk*

J

jamais *never*
jambe (f) *leg;* jambe cassée (f) *broken leg*
jambon (m) *ham*
janvier *January*
jardin (m) *garden, yard;* jardin public (m) *park*
jardinerie (f) *garden center*
jaune *yellow*
jazz (m) *jazz*
je *I;* je suis *I am;* je voudrais *I would like*
jeans (m pl) *jeans*
jeu (m) *game:* jeux vidéos (m pl) *computer games*
jeu de cartes (m) *pack of cards*
jeudi *Thursday*
jeune *young*
joli *nice; pretty* (place, etc.)
jouer *to play*
jouet (m) *toy*
jour (m) *day*
journal (m) *newspaper*
joyeux anniversaire! *happy birthday!*
juillet *July*

juin *June*
jupe (f) *skirt*
jupon (m) *slip*
jus (m) *juice:* jus d'orange *orange juice;* jus de fruit (m) *fruit juice*
jusqu'à *until*
juste *right; fair* (correct); ce n'est pas juste *it's not fair*
juste un peu *just a little*

K, L

kilo (m) *kilo*
kilomètre (m) *kilometer (0.62 miles)*
klaxon (m) *horn* (car)
la *the* (fem)
là *there;* il n'est pas là *he's out*
là-bas *over there*
lac (m) *lake*
lacet (m) *shoelace*
laid *ugly*
laine (f) *wool*
laisse (f) *lead*
lait (m) *milk*
lames de rasoir (f pl) *razor blades*
lampe (f) *lamp;* lampe de bureau *reading lamp;* lampe de chevet *bedside lamp;* lampe de poche (f) *flashlight*
landau (m) *baby carriage*
langouste (f) *crayfish* (saltwater)
langue (f) *language; tongue*
lapin (m) *rabbit*
laque (f) *hairspray*
large *wide*
lavabo (m) *basin* (sink)
laverie automatique (f) *laundromat*
lave-vaisselle (m) *dishwasher*
laxatif (m) *laxative*
le *the* (m)
leçon (f) *lesson*
lecteur de cassettes (m) *cassette player*
léger *light* (not heavy)
légumes (m pl) *vegetables*
lent *slow*
lentilles *lenses* (f pl); lentilles rigides *hard lenses;* lentilles semi-souples *gas-permeable lenses;* lentilles souples *soft lenses*
lequel, (fem) laquelle: lequel? *which?;* n'importe lequel *either of them*

les *the* (plural)
lessive(f) *laundry detergent*
lettre (f) *letter*
leur: leur chambre *their room;* leurs livres *their books*
levée (f) *mail pickup*
lever: se lever *to get up*
levier de vitesse (m) *gearshift*
librairie (f) *bookshop*
libre *free* (at liberty)
lime à ongles (f) *nail file*
limitation de vitesse (f) *speed limit*
limonade (f) *lemon soda*
linge (m) *laundry* (clothes)
lingettes (f pl) *baby wipes*
liqueur (f) *liqueur*
liquide: payer en liquide *to pay cash*
lire *to read*
liste (f) *list*
lit (m) *bed;* lit d'enfant (m) *crib*
littérature (f) *literature*
litre (m) *liter (quart)*
livraison (f) *delivery*
livre *book; pound* (weight)
loin *far*
long, (fem) longue *long*
longueur (f) *length*
lotion solaire (f) *suntan lotion*
louer *to rent*
lourd *heavy*
luge (f) *sled*
lumière (f) *light*
lundi *Monday*
lune (f) *moon;* lune de miel *honeymoon*
lunettes (f pl) *glasses;* lunettes de soleil *sunglasses*
Luxembourg (m) *Luxembourg*

M

ma: ma maison *my house*
machine à laver (f) *washing machine*
maçon (m) *bricklayer*
Madame *Mrs.*
Mademoiselle! *waitress!*
magasin (m) *shop;* magasin d'antiquités *antique shop*
magnétoscope (m) *VCR*
mai *May*
maigre *thin*
maillot de bain (m) *swimsuit; swimming trunks*

main (f) *hand*
maintenant *now*
mairie (f) *town hall*
mais *but*
maison (f) *house*
maître de conférences (m) *associate professor*
malade *ill*
mal à estomac (m) *stomachache*
mal à la tête (m) *headache*
mal de dents (m) *toothache*
mal de ventre (m) *stomachache*
manche (f) *sleeve*
Manche: la Manche *Channel*
mandarine (f) *tangerine*
manger *to eat*
manteau (m) *coat*
maquillage (m) *makeup*
marché (m) *market*
marcher *to walk*
mardi *Tuesday*
marée (f) *tide*
margarine (f) *margarine*
mari (m) *husband*
mariage (m) *wedding*
marié *married*
marmelade d'oranges (f) *marmalade*
marron *brown*
mars *March*
marteau (m) *hammer*
mascara (m) *mascara*
mât (m) *mast*
match (m) *match, game* (sport)
matelas (m) *mattress;* matelas pneumatique *air mattress*
matin (m) *morning*
mauvais *bad; poor* (bad quality); mauvais herbes (f) *weeds*
mécanicien (m) *mechanic*
médecin (m) *doctor*
médicaments (m pl) *medication*
médicine (m) *medicine* (subject)
Méditerranée: la Méditerranée (f) *Mediterranean*
méduse (f) *jellyfish*
meilleur: le meilleur *the best*
melon (m) *melon*
même *same;* le/la même ... *the same ...;* la même chose, s'il vous plaît *the same again, please*
menu (m) *set menu*
mer (f) *sea*

merci *thank you*
mercredi *Wednesday*
mère (f) *mother*
mes: mes chaussures *my shoes*
message (m) *message*
messagerie (f): messagerie électronique *email;* messagerie téléphonique *voicemail*
messe (f) *mass* (church)
métro (m) *underground*
mettre *to put*
meublé *furnished*
meubles (m pl) *furniture*
micro-ondes (m) *microwave*
midday *noon*
miel (m) *honey*
mieux *better*
milieu (m) *middle*
mince *thin*
minuit *midnight*
minute (f) *minute*
miroir (m) *mirror*
mobylette (f) *moped*
mode (f) *fashion*
modem (m) *modem*
moi *me;* c'est moi *it's me;* c'est pour moi; *it's for me;* c'est à moi *it's mine*
moins *less*
mois (m) *month*
mon: mon livre *my book*
moniteur (m) *monitor* (computer)
monnaie (f) *change* (money)
monsieur *sir;* Monsieur *Mr.*
montagne (f) *mountain*
montant de tente (m) *tent pole*
monter *to get on* (bus, etc.)
montre (f) *watch*
monument (m) *monument*
morceau (m) *piece*
mordre *to bite* (dog)
morsure (f) *bite* (by dog)
mort *dead*
mot (m) *word;* mot de passe (m) *password*
moteur (m) *engine* (car)
moto (f) *motorcycle*
mou *soft*
mouche (f) *fly* (insect)
mouchoir (m) *handkerchief*

mouchoirs *tissues*
mouillé *wet*
moules (f pl) *mussels*
mourir *to die*
mousse (f) *mousse* (hair); mousse à raser (f) *shaving foam*
moustache (f) *mustache*
moustique (m) *mosquito*
moutarde (f) *mustard*
mur (m) *wall* (outside)
mûr *ripe*
mûre (f) *blackberry*
musée (m) *museum;* musée d'art *art gallery*
musicien (m) *musician;* musicien des rues *street musician*
musique (f) *music;* musique classique *classical music;* musique folklorique *folk music;* musique pop *pop music*

N

nager *to swim*
natation (f) *swimming*
navette (pour aéroport) (f) *airport bus*
né(e): je suis né(e) en ... *I was born in ...*
nécessaire *necessary;* ce n'est pas nécessaire *that's not necessary*
négatif (m) *negative* (photo)
négociant en vins (m) *wine merchant*
neige (f) *snow*
neuf *nine*
neuf, (fem) neuve *new*
neveu (m) *nephew*
nez (m) *nose*
ni: ni un ni autre *neither of them;* ni ... ni ... *neither ... nor ...*
nièce (f) *niece*
nier *to deny*
noir *black*
noix (f) *nut* (fruit)
nom (m) *name;* nom de famille (m) *last name*
nombre (m) *number* (amount)
non *no*
nord (m) *north*
nos: nos enfants *our children*
notre: notre maison *our house*
nouer *to tie*
nourriture (f) *food*
nous *we;* nous deux *both of us;* nous

sommes *we are;* c'est à nous *it's ours;* c'est nous *it's us;* c'est pour nous *it's for us*
nouveau, (fem) nouvelle *new;* de nouveau *again*
nouvelles (f pl) *news*
novembre *November*
nudiste (m) *nudist*
nuit (f) *night*
nulle part *nowhere*
numéro (m) *number* (figure)

O

objectif (m) *lens* (camera)
objets trouvés (m pl) *lost property*
obturateur *shutter* (camera)
occupé *busy* (occupied)
octobre *October*
odeur (f) *smell*
œil (m) *eye*
œuf (m) *egg*
oignon (m) *onion*
oiseau (m) *bird*
olive (f) *olive*
omelette (f) *omelet*
oncle (m) *uncle*
ondulé *wavy* (hair)
ongle (m) *nail* (finger)
onze *eleven*
opérateur (m) *operator* (phone)
opération (f) *operation*
opticien (m) *optician*
or (m) *gold*
orage (m) *thunderstorm*
orange (f) *orange* (fruit, color)
orchestre (m) *orchestra*
ordinateur (m) *computer;* ordinateur portable (m) *laptop*
ordonnance (f) *prescription*
ordre du jour (m) *agenda*
ordures (f pl) *litter; garbage*
oreille (f) *ear*
oreiller (m) *pillow*
orgue (m) *organ* (music)
os (m) *bone*
ou *or*
où? *where?*
oublier *to forget*
ouest *west*
oui *yes*
ouvert (adj) *open*
ouvre-boîte (m) *can opener*
ouvrir *to open*

P

page (f) *page*
paiement (m) *payment*
pain (m) *bread;* pain grillé (m) *toast*
paire (f) *pair*
palais (m) *palace*
pâle *pale*
palmes (f pl) *flippers*
panier (m) *basket*
panne (f) *breakdown* (car); je suis tombé en panne *My car has broken down*
pansement (m) *plaster*
pantalon (m) *pants*
pantoufles (f pl) *slippers*
papa *dad*
papier (m) *paper;* papier à lettres *writing paper;* papier cadeau *gift wrap;* papier d'emballage *wrapping paper;* papier filtre *filter paper;* papier hygiénique *toilet paper*
paquet (m) *package, packet*
par: par avion *air mail;* par chemin de fer *by rail;* par exemple *for example;* par nuit *per night*
parapluie (m) *umbrella*
parasol (m) *sunshade*
parce que *because*
parcours de golf (m) *golf course*
pardon!, pardon? *excuse me!; sorry!* (apology); *pardon?*
pare-brise (m) *windscreen*
pare-chocs (m) *bumper*
parents (m pl) *parents*
paresseux *lazy*
parfait *perfect*
parfum (m) *perfume*
parking (m) *parking lot*
parler *to speak, talk;* parlez-vous ...? *do you speak ...?; ...* je ne parle pas ... *I don't speak*
paroi (f) *wall* (inside)
parterre de fleurs (m) *flowerbed*
parti (m) *party* (political)
particulièrement *especially*
partout *everywhere*
pas *not;* pas beaucoup *not many;* pas encore

not yet; il n'est pas ...
he's not ...

passage (m) *driveway*

passager (m)
passenger

passeport (m) *passport;*
passeport d'animaux
(m) *pet passport*

passe-temps (m)
hobby

pastilles pour la gorge
(f pl) *throat pastilles*

pâtes (f pl) *pasta*

patinoire (f) *ice rink*

patins à glace (m pl)
ice skates

pâtisserie (f) *bakery,
pastry shop*

pauvre *poor* (not rich)

payer *to pay*

pays (m) *country*
(state); pays de
Galles (m) *Wales*

pêche (f) *peach;
fishing;* aller à la
pêche *to go fishing*

peigne (m) *comb*

peigner *to comb*

peinture (f) *paint;
painting*

pelle (f) *spade*
(shovel)

pellicule couleur (f)
color film

pelouse (f) *lawn*

pendant *during*

pendule (f) *clock*

penser *to think*

pension complète (f)
full board

père (m) *father*

perle (f) *pearl*

permanente (f) *perm*

permis (m) *license;*
permis de conduire
(m) *driver's license*

personne *nobody*

petit *small*

petit ami (m)
boyfriend

petit déjeuner (m)
breakfast

petite amie (f)
girlfriend

petite-fille (f)
granddaughter

petit-fils (m)
grandson

petits pois (m pl) *peas*

pétrole (m) *paraffin*

peut-être *maybe;
perhaps*

phares (m pl)
headlights

pharmacie (f)
pharmacy

photo (f) *photograph*

photographe (m/f)
photographer

photographier *to
photograph*

piano (m) *piano*

pickpocket (m)
pickpocket

pièce (f) *coin; play*
(theatre)

pièces de rechange
(f pl) *spare parts*

pied (m) *foot*

piéton (m)
pedestrian

pile (f) *battery*
(flashlight)

pilote (m) *pilot*

pince (f): pince à
épiler *tweezers;* pince
à linge *peg;* pince à
ongles *nail clippers*

pinceau (m)
paintbrush

pipe (f) *pipe* (for
smoking)

pique *spades* (cards)

pique-nique (m) *picnic*

piquer *to bite* (snake),
sting (insect)

piquet de tente (m)
tent peg

piqûre (f) *bite* (snake);
sting (insect);
injection

pire *worse, worst*

piscine (f) *swimming
pool*

piste (f) *runway;
ski slope;* piste pour
débutants *beginners'
slope*

pistolet (m) *pistol*

piston (m) *piston*

pizza (f) *pizza*

placard (m) *cabinet*

place (f) *room* (space);
seat; square (in
town)

plafond (m) *ceiling*

plage(f) *beach*

plaisanterie (f) *joke*

plan (m) *town map*

plancher (m) *floor*
(ground)

plan de travail (m)
countertop

plancher (m) *floor*
(ground)

plante (f) *plant*

plaque
d'immatriculation (f)
license plate

plastique (m) *plastic*

plat *flat* (level)

plateau (m) *tray*

plats (m pl) *main
courses;* plats préparés
(m pl) *prepared
meals*

pleurer *to cry* (weep)

plombage (m) *filling*
(in tooth)

plombier (m) *plumber*

plongeoir (m) *diving
board*

plonger *to dive*

pluie (f) *rain*

plus *more:* plus de
more than; plus tard
later; plus ou moins
more or less

plusieurs *several*

plutôt *quite*

pneu (m) *tire;* pneu
crevé (m) *flat tire*

poche (f) *pocket*

poêle (f) *frying pan*

poignée (f) *handle*
(door)

poignet (m) *wrist*

poire (f) *pear*

poireaux (m) *leek*

poison (m) *poison*

poisson (m) *fish*

poissonnerie (f)
fishmonger

poitrine (f) *chest*

poivre (m) *pepper*
(and salt)

poivron (m) *pepper*
(red/green)

police (f) *police*

policier (m) *police
officer*

politique (f) *politics*

pommade (f) *ointment*

pomme (f) *apple*

pomme de terre (f)
potato

pont (m) *bridge*

porc (m) *pork*

porcelaine (f) *china*

port (m) *harbor; port*

porte (f) *door*
(building); porte
d'embarquement (f)
gate (at airport)

porte-bagages (m)
luggage rack

portefeuille (m)
wallet

porte-monnaie (m)
purse

porteur (m) *porter*

portière (f) *car door*

porto (m) *port* (drink)

possible *possible;* dès
que possible *as soon
as possible*

poste (f) *mail; post
office*

poster (m) *poster*
(inside); (verb)
to post

pot d'echappement (m)
exhaust (car)

poubelle (f) *garbage
can, trash can*

poudre (f) *powder*

poulet (m) *chicken*

poupée (f) *doll*

pour *for;* pour moi *for
me;* pour une semaine
for a week

pourboire (m) *tip*
(money)

pourquoi? *why?*
pousser *to push*
poussette (f) *stroller*
pouvoir *to be able;* je peux avoir ...? *can I have ...?;* vous pouvez ...? *can you ...?*
préférer *to prefer*
premier *first;* premier étage (m) *first floor;* première classe *first class;* premiers soins (m pl) *first aid*
prendre *to take;* prendre le train *take the train;* prendre un bain *take a bath*
prénom (m) *first name*
près de *near;* près de la porte *near the door;* près de la fenêtre *by the window*
préservatif (m) *condom*
presque *almost*
pressé: je suis pressé *I'm in a hurry*
pressing (m) *dry-cleaner*
prêt *ready*
prêtre (m) *priest*
prie: je vous en prie *you're welcome*
printemps (m) *spring (season)*
prise (f) *plug (electrical);* prise multiple *adapter*
prise de sang (f) *blood test*
privé *private*
prix (m) *price;* prix d'entrée *admission charge;* prix du billet (m) *fare*
problème (m) *problem*
prochain *next;* la semaine prochaine *next week*
produit pour la vaisselle (m) *dishwashing liquid*
produits de beauté (m pl) *cosmetics*
produits entretien (m pl) *household products*
produits laitiers (m pl) *dairy products*
produits surgelés (m pl) *frozen foods*
professeur (m) *professor; teacher (secondary)*
profession (f) *profession*
profond *deep*
promener: aller se promener *to go for a walk*
propre (adj) *clean*

prudent *careful;* soyez prudent! *be careful!*
public (m) *public*
puce (f) *flea*
pull (m) *sweater*
punaise (f) *thumbtack*
pyjama (m) *pajamas*

Q

quai (m) *dock; platform*
qualité (f) *quality*
quand? *when?*
quarante *forty*
quart (m) *quarter*
quatorze *fourteen*
quatre *four*
quatre-vingt *eighty*
quatre-vingt-dix *ninety*
quatrième *fourth*
que *than*
quel âge avez-vous? *how old are you?*
quelle heure est-il? *what's the time?*
quelque chose *something*
quelque part *somewhere*
quelquefois *sometimes*
quelqu'un *somebody*
quelqu'un d'autre *someone else*
qu'est-ce que c'est? *what's that?; what is it?*
question (f) *question*
queue (f) *line*
qui? *who?*
quincaillerie (f) *hardware shop*
quinze *fifteen;* quinze jours *two weeks*

R

radiateur (m) *heater; radiator*
radio (f) *X-ray; radio*
radis (m) *radish*
rafraîchissements (m pl) *refreshments*
raie (f) *parting (in hair)*
raisin (m) *grape;* raisin sec (m) *raisin*
rallonge (f) *extension lead*
ramer *to row*
rames (f pl) *oars*
randonée (f) *hiking*
rapide *fast; quick*
rapport de police (m) *police report*
rare *rare (uncommon)*
raser: se raser *to shave*
rat (m) *rat*
râteau (m) *rake*
rayon (m) *aisle (supermarket)*
réception (f) *reception*

receptionniste (m/f) *receptionist*
réclamation de bagages (f) *baggage claim*
recommandé: en recommandé *registered mail*
record (m) *record (sports, etc.)*
reçu (m) *receipt*
réduction (f) *discount*
regarde: cela ne vous regarde pas *it's none of your business*
regarder *to watch*
règle (f) *ruler*
rein (m) *kidney*
religion (f) *religion*
remercier *to thank*
remonte-pente (m) *ski lift*
remorque (f) *trailer*
rendez-vous (m) *appointment*
rendre *to return (give back);* rendre visite *visit (person)*
repas (m) *meal*
repasser *to iron*
répondeur (m) *answering machine*
reposer: se reposer *to rest (relax)*
reseignments (m pl) *directory (telephone)*
réservation (f) *reservation*
réserver *to book, reserve*
résistant *strong (material)*
respirer *to breathe*
ressort (m) *spring (mechanical)*
restaurant (m) *restaurant*
reste (m) *rest (remainder)*
retard (m) *delay*
retirer *to withdraw*
rétroviseur (m) *car mirror*
réunion (f) *meeting*
réveil (m) *alarm clock*
revenir *to return (come back)*
revue (f) *magazine*
rez-de-chaussée (m) *ground floor*
rhum (m) *rum*
rhume (m) *cold (illness);* rhume des foins (m) *hay fever*
riche *rich*
rideau (m) *curtain*
rien *nothing;* ça ne fait rien *it doesn't matter*
rire *to laugh*
rivière (f) *river*
riz (m) *rice*
robe (f) *dress*

robinet (m) *tap* (water)
rocher (m) *rock* (stone)
rock (m) *rock* (music)
roman (m) *novel*
rond *round* (circular)
rondelle (f) *washer*
rond-point (m) *roundabout, rotary*
room service (m) *room service*
rose (f) *rose; pink* (adj)
rôti *roasted*
roue (f) *wheel*
rouge *red;* rouge à lèvres (m) *lipstick*
rougeur (f) *rash*
rouleaux (m pl) *curlers*
roux *red* (of hair)
rue (f) *street*
rugby (m) *rugby*
ruines (f pl) *ruins*
ruisseau (m) *stream* (small river)

S

sa: sa maison *his/her house*
sable (m) *sand*
sac (m) *bag;* sac à dos *backpack;* sac à main *handbag;* sac de couchage *sleeping bag;* sac poubelle *trash can liner*
saignant *rare* (steak)
salade (f) *lettuce; salad*
salle (f) *room;* salle à manger *dining room;* salle d'attente *waiting room;* salle d'opérations *operating room;* salle de bains *bathroom;* salle de conférences *conference room;* salle de radiology *X-ray departments;* salle des urgences *emergency room*
salon (m) *living room*
salut *hi*
samedi *Saturday*
sandales (f pl) *sandals*
sandwich (m) *sandwich*
sang (m) *blood*
sans *without;* sans plomb *unleaded*
santé! *cheers!*
s'arrêter *to stop*
sauce (f) *sauce*
saucisse (f) *sausage*
saumon (m) *salmon*
sauna (m) *sauna*
savoir *to know* (fact); je ne sais pas *I don't know*

savon (m) *soap*
science (f) *science*
seau (m) *bucket*
sec, (fem) sèche *dry*
sèche-cheveux (m) *hairdryer*
seconde (f) *second* (of time)
seconde: en seconde *second class*
secrétaire (m/f) *secretary*
secteur (m) *field* (academic)
sécurité: en sécurité *safe* (not in danger)
seize *sixteen*
sel (m) *salt*
semaine (f) *week*
séminaire (m) *seminar*
sentir *to smell*
séparé (adj) *separate*
séparer *to separate*
sept *seven*
septembre *September*
sérieux *serious*
seringue (f) *syringe*
séropositif(ve) *HIV-positive*
serveur (m) *waiter*
serveuse (f) *waitress*
service de pédiatrie (m) *children's ward*
serviette (f) *towel*
serviettes hygiéniques (f pl) *sanitary napkins*
ses: ses chaussures *his/her shoes*
seul *alone; single* (one)
seulement *only*
shampooing (m) *shampoo*
short (m) *shorts*
si *if; whether*
SIDA *AIDS*
siège pour bébé (m) *car seat* (for a baby)
siège social (m) *headquarters*
silencieux *quiet* (person)
s'il vous plaît *please*
simple *simple*
sirop (m) *syrup*
site web (m) *website*
six *six*
ski (m) *ski;* faire du ski *to go skiing*
skier *to ski*
slip (m) *underpants*
snack (m) *snack*
sœur(f) *sister*
soie (f) *silk*
soif: j'ai soif *I'm thirsty*
soir (m) *evening;* ce soir *tonight*
soirée (f) *party* (get together)

soit ... soit ... *either ... or ...*
soixante *sixty*
soixante-dix *seventy*
soldes (f pl) *sale* (at reduced prices)
soleil (m) *sun*
solution de trempage (f) *soaking solution* (for contact lenses)
sommeil (m) *sleep*
somnifère (m) *sleeping pill*
son livre *his/her book*
sonnette (f) *bell* (door)
sortie (f) *exit*
sortie de secours (f) *emergency exit*
sortir *to leave*
soucoupe (f) *saucer*
soûl *drunk*
soupape (f) *valve*
soupe (f) *soup*
souper (m) *supper*
sourcil (m) *eyebrow*
sourd *deaf*
sourire (m) *smile; smile* (verb)
souris (f) *mouse*
sous ... *below ...; under ...*
sous-sol (m) *basement*
sous-vêtements (f pl) *underwear*
soutien-gorge (m) *bra*
souvenir (m) *souvenir; remember* (verb); je m'en souviens *I remember;* je ne me souviens pas *I don't remember*
souvent *often*
sport(m) *sport*
stade (m) *stadium*
stagiaire (m) *trainee*
station (f) *metro station*
station de ski (f) *ski resort*
station-service (f) *gas station*
statue (f) *statue*
steak (m) *steak*
store (m) *blind* (window)
stupide *stupid*
stylo (m) *pen;* stylo-bille (m) *ballpoint pen;* stylo-plume (m) *fountain pen*
sucette (f) *lollipop*
sucre (m) *sugar*
sucré *sweet* (not sour)
sud (m) *south*
suisse(sse) *Swiss*
Suisse: la Suisse *Switzerland*
supermarché (m) *supermarket*
supplément (m) *supplement*

suppositoire (m)
suppository

sur ... *on* ...

sûr *sure*

survêtement (m)
jogging suit

sweat-shirt (m)
sweatshirt

sympathique *nice*
(person)

synagogue (f)
synagogue

syndicat d'initiative (m)
tourist office

T

ta: ta maison *your
house* (singular
informal)

tabac (m) *tobacco;
tobaconnist*

table (f) *table*

tablette de chocolat (f)
bar of chocolate

taille (f) *size*

taille-crayon (m) *pencil
sharpener*

talc (m) *talcum
powder*

talon (m) *heel*

tampon (m) *tampon*

tante (f) *aunt*

tapis (m) *carpet;* tapis
de sol (m)
groundsheet

tapisserie (f) *tapestry*

tard *late;* bus est en
retard *the bus is late*

tasse (f) *cup; mug*

taux de change (m)
exchange rate

taxi (m) *taxi*

télé câblée (f) *cable
TV*

téléphérique (m) *cable
car*

téléphone (m)
telephone; téléphone
portable (m) *cell
phone*

téléphoner *to telephone*
(verb)

télévision (f) *television*

témoin (m) *witness*

température (f)
temperature

tempête (f) *storm;*
tempête de neige (f)
blizzard

temps (m) *weather;
time;* de temps en
temps *occasionally*

tennis (m) *tennis;* les
tennis (m pl) *athletic
shoes*

tente (f) *tent*

terminal (m) *terminal*

terrain de camping (m)
campground

terrasse (f) *terrace*

terre (f) *land; soil*

tes: tes chaussures
your shoes (singular
informal; plural
noun)

tête (f) *head*

thé (m) *tea*

théâtre (m) *theater*

ticket (m) *ticket*
(underground, bus)

timbre (m) *stamp*

tire-bouchon (m)
corkscrew

tirer *to pull*

tiroir (m) *drawer*

tissu (m) *material*

toboggan (m)
toboggan

toi: c'est à toi *it's yours*

toilettes (f pl)
restrooms

toit (m) *roof*

tomate (f) *tomato*

ton: ton livre *your book*
(singular informal)

tondeuse à gazon (f)
lawnmower

tongs (f pl) *flip-flops*

tonic (m) *tonic*

torchon (m) *dish cloth*

tôt *early*

toucher *to feel, touch*

toujours *always*

tour (f) *tower*

tourism (m)
sightseeing

touriste (m/f) *tourist*

tourne-disque (m)
record player

tournevis (m)
screwdriver

tous les deux *both of
them*

tousser *to cough*

tout *all; everything;*
tout droit *straight
ahead;* tout le monde
everyone; tout seul
all alone

toux (f) *cough*

tracteur (m) *tractor*

tradition (f) *tradition*

traducteur (m)
translator

traduire *to translate*

train (m) *train*

tranquille *quiet*
(street, etc.)

transpiration (f) *sweat*

transpirer *to sweat*

travail (m) *job; work*

travailler *to work*

traverser *to cross*

trèfle *clubs* (cards)

treize *thirteen*

trente *thirty*

très *very*

tricoter *knit*

triste *sad*

trois *three*

troisième *third*

trop *too* (excessively)

trottoir (m) *sidewalk*

tu *you* (singular
informal); tu es *you
are*

tunnel (m) *tunnel;* le
tunnel sous La Manche
Channel Tunnel

tuyau (m) *pipe* (for
water)

U

un/une *a; one;* un/une
autre *another*
(different)

université (f) *university*

urgence (f) *emergency*

urgent *urgent*

utensiles de cuisine
(f pl) *cooking utensils*

utile *useful*

utiliser *to use*

V

vacances (m pl)
vacation

vaccination (f)
vaccination

vague (f) *wave;* faint
(adj)

valise (f) *case*

valise (f) *suitcase*

vallée (f) *valley*

vanille (f) *vanilla*

vapeur: à la vapeur
steamed

vase (m) *vase*

veau (m) *veal*

végétarien (adj)
vegetarian

véhicule (m) *vehicle*

vélo (m) *bicycle;* vélo
tout terrain (m)
mountain bike

vendre *to sell*

vendredi *Friday*

venir *to come;* je viens
de ... *I come from ...*

vent (m) *wind*

vente (f) *sale*
(transaction)

ventilateur (m) *fan*
(ventilator)

vernis à ongles (m)
nail polish

verre (m) *glass*

verres de contact (f pl)
contact lenses

verrou (m) *bolt* (on
door)

verrouiller *to bolt*

vert *green*

veste (f) *jacket*

vêtements (m pl)
clothes

vétérinaire (m)
veterinarian

viande (f) *meat*

vide *empty*

vidéo (f) *video* (film/tape)

vie (f) *life*

vieux, (fem) vieille *old*

villa (f) *villa*

village (m) *village*

ville (f) *city; town*

vin (m) *wine*

vinaigre (m) *vinegar*

vingt *twenty*

violet *purple*

violon (m) *violin*

vis (f) *screw*

visage (m) *face*

viseur (m) *viewfinder*

visite (f) *tour; visit*

visiter *to visit* (place)

visiteur (m) *visitor*

vitesse (f) *gear* (car); *speed*

vodka (f) *vodka*

voile (f) *sailing*

voilier (m) *sailboat*

voir *to see;* je vois *I see;* je ne vois rien *I can't see anything*

voiture (f) *car; train car*

voix (f) *voice*

vol (m) *flight*

volaille (f) *poultry*

volant (m) *steering wheel*

voler *to fly; steal;* on a volé *it's been stolen*

volet (m) *shutter* (window)

voleur (m) *thief*

vomir *to be sick* (vomit)

vos: vos chaussures *your shoes* (singular formal; plural; plural noun)

votre: votre maison *your house* (singular formal; plural; singular noun)

vouloir *to want;* je veux *I want;* vous voulez? *do you want?*

vous *you* (singular formal; plural); vous êtes *you are*

voyage (m) trip, *journey*

vrai *true*

vue (f) *view*

W, Y, Z

wagon-lit (m) *sleeper car* (train)

wagon-restaurant (m) *restaurant car* (train)

whisky (m) *whiskey*

yaourt (m) *yogurt*

yeux (m pl) *eyes*

zoo (m) *zoo*

Acknowledgments

The publisher would like to thank the following for their help in the preparation of this book: Anne-Marie Miller for the organization of location photography in France; Hôtel-Restaurant, "Le Rabelais," Fontenay le Comte; Gare Routière de Fontenay le Comte; Pharmacie Parot, Nieul Sur L'Autise; Garage Gouband, Oulmes; Musée de l'Abbaye de Nieul Sur L'Autise (Cabinet Tetrac, Nantes); Boulangerie des familles, Coulon; Fromagerie, rue St Marthe, Niort; Fruits et Primeurs Benoit, Halles de Niort; Gare SNCF de Niort; Magnet Showroom, Enfield, MyHotel, London; Kathy Gammon; Julliette Meeus and Harry.

Language content for Dorling Kindersley by G-AND-W PUBLISHING
Managed by **Jane Wightwick**
Editing and additional input: **Pamela Wightwick, Christine Arthur, Leila Gaafar**

Additional design assistance: **Lee Riches, Fehmi Cömert, Sally Geeve**
Additional editorial assistance: **Paul Docherty, Lynn Bresler**
Picture research: **Louise Thomas**

Picture credits

Key:
t=top; b=bottom; l=left; r=right; c=center; A=above; B=below

p2 **Alamy:** *Ian Dagnall; p4/5* **Alamy:** *f1 Online tl; images-of-france tr;* **Alamy RF:** *Andy Marshall bl;* **DK Images:** *br; Neil Lukas tcr; p6/7* **Laura Knox:** *cl; p10/12* **Alamy RF:** *BananaStock cAr; RubberBall bl;* **Ingram Image Library:** *bl; p12/13* **Alamy RF:** *John Foxx cAr; RubberBall br;* **DK Images:** *cl; Steve Shott cBr;* **Ingram Image Library:** *tr; p14/15* **Alamy:** *images-of-france tr;* **Ingram Image Library:** *cAl, cl, cBl, cAr, cBr, bcr; p16/17* **Alamy RF:** *RubberBall bcr;* **Ingram Image Library:** *tr; p18/19* **DK Images:** *David Murray tr; Ian O'Leary clB; p22/23* **DK Images:** *cl, Andy Crawford cAr; Susanna Price br; Magnus Rew tcrB;* **Ingram Image Library:** *bcl, tcr; p24/25* **DK Images:** *clA, Dave King tr; p26/27* **Ingram Image Library:** *cl; p28/29* **DK Images:** *Andy Crawford tcr; Dave King cr; Matthew Ward bclA;* **Ingram Image Library:** *bcrA, bcr; p30/31* **Alamy RF:** *Comstock Images bcl;* **DK Images:** *cl, bclA; p36/37* **DK Images:** *bcl, bcr;* **Ingram Image Library:** *bl; p38/39* **Alamy RF:** *Imageshop / Zefa Visual Media cl; p40/41* **Alamy:** *images-of-france bl;* **Alamy RF:** *Justin Kase cAr;* **DK Images:** *cl, bcr; p42/43* **Alamy:** *Artografika Bildagentur cr;* **Alamy RF:** *Image Source cAr; Andy Marshall cAr; p44/45* *Courtesy of* **Renault:** *c; p46/47* **Alamy:** *Artografika Bildagentur cr; images-of-france cl;* **Alamy RF:** *Imageshop / Zefa Visual Media br;* **DK Images:** *bcl;* **Ingram Image Library:** *trlB; Courtesy of* **Renault:** *tcr; p48/49* **Alamy:** *Agence Images tcr; Ian Dagnell c; PCL bcr; Peter Titmuss cr;* **DK Images:** *bcl; p50/51* **Alamy:** *Robert Harding Picture Library c; p52/53* **Alamy:** *imagebroker tcr;* **Alamy RF:** *Image Farm Inc cAr; Photov.com / Hisham Ibrahim tcrB;* **DK Images:** *cl; p54/55* **Alamy:** *Frank Herholdt bcl; Jackson Smith cBl;* **Alamy RF:** *BananaStock cl; John Foxx c; Image Source cAr; ThinkStock cl;* **DK Images:** *Andy Crawford bclA; p56/57* **Alamy:** *Agence Images clA; Ian Dagnell cl; PCL tl; Peter Titmuss cAl;* **DK Images:** *clAA; Courtesy of* **Renault:** *bc; p58/59* **Alamy:** *Michael Juno tcr;* **Alamy RF:** *Brand X Pictures cBl, cBBl; Image Source cAl;* **DK Images:** *cAl; p60/61* **Alamy:** *Robert Harding Picture Library bcr;* **Alamy RF:** *Image Source cAr;* **DK Images:** *Steve Gorton bl, tcrB; Pia Tryde cAAr;* **Ingram Image Library:** *cr; p62/63* **DK Images:** *Stephen Whitehorn c; p64/65* **Alamy:** *Arcaid bcrA;* **Alamy RF:** *GKPhotography cBr; Goodshoot cAAr; imagebroker c; Justin Kase tcrB;* **DK Images:** *Steve Tanner cAr;* **Ingram Image Library:** *tcr; p66/67* **Alamy:** *Arcaid tl;* **Alamy RF:** *Image Source cr;* **DK Images:** *Stephen Whitehorn bl;* **Ingram Image Library:** *br; p68/69* **Alamy:** *Balearic Pictures cr; f1 Online cBl; Doug Houghton cl; Indiapicture clB;* **Alamy RF:** *images-of-france cBr; Justin Kase bl;* **DK Images:** *Peter Wilson cAl; p72/73* **Alamy RF:** *imagebroker tcrB; Image Source cAr; Comstock Images cr;* **Avery Weight-Tronix:** *bl; p74/75* **Alamy RF:** *Doug Norman bl;* **Ingram Image Library:** *c; p76/77* **Alamy:** *Balearic Pictures cl; f1 Online clB; Indiapicture bl;* **DK Images:** *Peter Wilson cAl; p80/81* **Getty:** *Taxi / Rob Melnychuk bc;* **Ingram Image Library:** *cAr; Xerox UK Ltd:* *cr; p82/83* **Alamy:** *wildphotos.com cAr;* **Alamy RF:** *FogStock cAAl; Momentum Creative Group cAl; Shoosh / Up the Res cBl;* **Ingram Image Library:** *cl; p84/85* **Alamy:** *Brand X Pictures cr; f1 Online c;* **Alamy RF:** *BananaStock bcl; SuperStock tr;* **Ingram Image Library:** *cAr; p86/87* **Getty:** *Taxi / Rob Melnychuk tc; p90/91* **Alamy RF:** *Brand X Pictures tr;* **DK Images:** *cl; David Jordan cr; Stephen Oliver cr;* **Ingram Image Library:** *cBr; p82/93* **Alamy RF:** *Pixland cr;* **DK Images:** *cl; Guy Ryecart tr;* **Ingram Image Library:** *br; p94/95* **Alamy:** *David Kamm cl; Phototake Inc bcl;* **Alamy RF:** *Comstock Images cr; ImageState Royalty Free cr;* **DK Images:** *Stephen Oliver tcr; p96/97* **Alamy RF:** *Pixland br;* **DK Images:** *tl;* **Ingram Image Library:** *tr; p98/99* **Alamy RF:** *Bildagentur Franz Waldhaeusl bl; ThinkStock br;* **DK Images:** *Peter Kindersley cr;* **Getty RF:** *Photodisc Green c p100/101* **DK Images:** *Steve Gorton tr; p102/103* **Alamy:** *The Garden Picture Library tcr; cAAr; Hortus b; D Hurst tcrB;* **Ingram Image Library:** *cAr; p104/105* **DK Images:** *Paul Bricknell cl(6); Jane Burton bcl; Geoff Dann cl(2); Max Gibbs cl(4); Frank Greenaway cl(3); Dave King cl(1), cAr; Tracy Morgan c(5); p106/107* **Alamy:** *The Garden Picture Library br;* **DK Images:** *Peter Kindersley cr; p110/111* **Alamy RF:** *RubberBall cr;* **DK Images:** *Andy Crawford cl; p112/113* **Alamy RF:** *Image Source cl;* **DK Images:** *bl; p114/115* **Alamy RF:** *Image Source cr; f1 Online cl; Ingram Image Library:* *bcr; p116/117* **Alamy:** *The Garden Picture Library cAl; p118/119* **DK Images:** *Steve Gorton tcr;* **GettyNews:** *Giuseppe Cacace c; p120/121* **Alamy:** *ImageState / Pictor International cl;* **Alamy RF:** *Sarkis Images tcr;* **DK Images:** *cbl, bcl; Kevin Mallett br; p122/123* **Alamy RF:** *BananaStock cbr; p124/125* **Alamy:** *ImageState / Pictor International bclA;* **DK Images:** *cBl, bcl; Paul Bricknell tc(5); Geoff Dann tc(3); Max Gibbs tc(2); Frank Greenaway tc(2); Dave King tc(4); Kevin Mallett bl; Tracy Morgan tc(6); p126/127* **Alamy:** *imagebroker clB;* **Alamy RF:** *© Hisham Ibrahim / Photov.com blA; Image Farm Inc bl; p128* **DK Images:** *Neil Mersh.*

All other images **Mike Good**.